Cognitive Behavioral Therapy Course Made Simple

Overcome Anxiety, insomnia and Depression, Break Negative Thought Patterns, Maintain Mindfulness, and Retrain Your Brain through the most Effective Psychotherapy

By

Daniel Wallaces

Table of Contents

Introduction 6

Part 1: Understanding Cognitive Behavioral Therapy 9

    The Principles of Cognitive Behavioral Therapy 10

    How Cognitive Behavioral Therapy Works 18

Part 2: Identifying Problems in Your Life 23

    The Basics of Anxiety and Depression 24

    Principles of Automatic and Intrusive Thoughts............ 43

    Understanding the 'Thinking-Feeling-Acting' Connection 48

Part 3: Getting Back Control of Your Life 54

    How to Set Practical and Meaningful Goals 55

    The Golden Rules of Goal Setting... 62

    Are Your Goals Really Yours?.. 69

Cracking Your Pessimistic and Intrusive Thoughts 79

    Reshaping Your Attitude for a Positive Mindset............ 87

Becoming Your Own Positivity Hero 95

Recognizing and Modifying Your Core Beliefs 102

Maintaining Positive Mindfulness 108

Easy Ways to Live a More Positively Driven Life 126

Dealing with Negativity: Fear, Worry, Anxiety, Procrastination, etc. 136

Erase Negativity with Mini Habits 152

Conclusion 156

© Copyright 2018 by ___Daniel Wallaces___ - All rights reserved.

The following eBook is reproduced below with the goal of providing information that is as accurate and as reliable as possible. Regardless, purchasing this eBook can be seen as consent to the fact that both the publisher and the author of this book are in no way experts on the topics discussed within, and that any recommendations or suggestions made herein are for entertainment purposes only. Professionals should be consulted as needed before undertaking any of the action endorsed herein.

This declaration is deemed fair and valid by both the American Bar Association and the Committee of Publishers Association and is legally binding throughout the United States.

Furthermore, the transmission, duplication, or reproduction of any of the following work, including precise information, will be considered an illegal act, irrespective of whether it is done electronically or in print. The legality extends to creating a secondary or tertiary copy of the work or a recorded copy and is only allowed with an expressed written consent of the Publisher. All additional rights are reserved.

The information in the following pages is broadly considered a truthful and accurate account of facts, and as such, any inattention, use, or misuse of the information in question by the reader will render any resulting actions solely under their purview. There are no scenarios in which the publisher or the original author of this work can be in any fashion deemed liable for any hardship or damages that may befall them after undertaking information described herein.

Additionally, the information found on the following pages is intended for informational purposes only and should thus be considered, universal. As befitting its nature, the information presented is without assurance regarding its continued validity or interim quality. Trademarks that mentioned are done without written consent and can in no way be considered an endorsement from the trademark holder.

Introduction

Welcome to the *Cognitive Behavioral Therapy Guide & Workbook Made Simple*!

Todays' world is, well, *HECTIC*. From the hustle and bustle of our own daily lives to reading and seeing negativity hit our television screens, it always seems as if the world is out to get us and we can never quite catch that much-deserved break.

As you can imagine, anxiety, depression, and negativity can easily take root and grow within us, making us just the shell of the people we truly are. Life has a way of getting us down, but our life's worth lies in the way that we defeat these negative thoughts and actions, make the best out of what one is provided with and live our lives to the fullest.

I know what you are thinking; *"Pffft. Easier said than done."*

STOP. Don't close this book yet. If you are looking for methods to strengthen your armor against the darkness in life, then you have come to the proper place to become prepared for battle against negativity!

I'm sure you have heard multiple times that having a positive mindset can drastically change the course of your life. However, when the going gets tough, it can be hard to see the light in hard situations and know what actions to take to make the most of the cards you are dealt.

Negativity is thrown at us on a daily basis, whether it is a rude customer, a mean boss, or terrible things happening in your relationships. Everyday life can be a drag.

Have you ever heard of the abbreviation CBT? If not, it stands for Cognitive Behavioral Therapy. I certainly don't blame you for cringing at the word 'therapy'. Trust me; I do too. However, CBT is an entirely different take on therapy, as it is centered on adjusting our mind to learn how to see the things we experience in life differently.

CBT is a method of psychotherapy that emphasizes on the role that our minds play in how we feel and how we act.

The chapters of this book will:

- Teach you what cognitive behavioral therapy is and how it works

- Who will best benefit from learning about this form of therapy

- Ways to identify areas of your life that breed negativity

- Many unique methods that will help better your life for the long-term

Thanks again for joining me on this journey to a better, more positive life! Every effort was made to ensure it is full of as much useful information as possible.

Part 1: Understanding Cognitive Behavioral Therapy

The Principles of Cognitive Behavioral Therapy

What is Cognitive Behavioral Therapy (CBT)?

CBT, or cognitive behavioral therapy, is a form of therapy that looks deeper into the links between one's thoughts, emotions, and behaviors. It is a short-term type of therapy, as it is directive and structured in its approach to help treat mental disorders.

The idea behind cognitive behavioral therapy is to lessen the distress that patients experience by developing adaptive cognitions and behaviors. It is very widely researched, which makes it a supportive method in psychotherapy. There is a strong clinical evidence to back these findings, which is why CBT is a highly recommended treatment option for common mental health ailments that people suffer from.

In Layman's term, the core idea behind the cognitive behavioral therapy is centered on the hypothesis that the way people think and act is influenced by their perceptions of life and events they live through. It is not a situation itself that determines what someone feels, but rather the method in which they construct that scenario.

Principles of Cognitive Behavioral Therapy

- Based on a cognitive model that comes from emotional responses

1. Brief and time-limited
2. Therapeutic relationships with a sound foundation are necessary for the best therapy
3. Based on an effort that is collaborative between patients and therapist(s)
4. Based on the aspect of Stoic philosophy
5. Utilizes the Socratic Method
6. Is directive and structured in nature
7. Based on educational models and findings
8. The theory of CBT relies on the Inductive Method

Cognitive behavioral therapy is not a distinct therapeutic technique. In fact, CBT is a generalized term for a larger classification of therapies and the similarities they have. There are multiple approaches to CBT, such as:

- Dialectic behavioral therapy

- Cognitive therapy

- Rational living therapy

- Rational behavior therapy

- Emotive behavior therapy

The foundation of CBT is based on the cognitive portions of emotional responses.

This type of therapy stands strong on the foundational fact that our thoughts are what cause us to feel and act in certain ways, not just external things such as events and people. The best thing about this is that *we can change* the way we think, feel, and act, even if a situation we are living through will never change.

CBT is a Time-Limited and Briefer Therapy.

CBT is one of the most rapid forms of therapy in existence today, unlike other forms of therapy, such as psychoanalysis, which can take years.

CBT is briefer thanks to its highly instructive nature, and that it makes good use of people's homework assignments that therapists give them. It is very limited on time, which helps patients to better understand from the beginning that there will be a point when this therapy will end. CBT is not open-ended and a process that never has a true ending.

A Strong Therapeutic Relationship is Needed for Effective CBT

Many other forms of therapy are assumed to be great for patients because of the positive relationship patients have with their therapist(s). However, in CBT, therapists know that a good, trusting relationship is not the focus of getting better.

They believe that patients change because they gain the knowledge on how to think and act differently in stressful and/or negative situations. This is why the focus of CBT therapists is to teach self-counseling skills to their patients.

CBT is a Collaborative Effort

Therapists in cognitive behavioral therapy desire to acquire what their patients want out of their lives and then take the steps needed for them to reach those goals.

The therapist's in CBT listen, teach, and encourage their patients, which the patient's main role is to openly express their concerns, learn, and then utilize what they have learned in everyday scenarios.

Stoic Philosophy is the Foundation of CBT.

Not every approach to cognitive behavioral therapy goes to emphasize stoicism. CBT doesn't teach patients to tell others how they should feel. However, those that seek therapy in the first place do not want to feel a certain negative way any longer.

This is where stoicism comes into play, for it teaches patients to feel calmer when they are confronted with situations that are not desirable and/or stressful. It doesn't matter how we act, there will always be negative situations.

You can either be upset about the problems you are facing or try to have a better outlook to erase as many issues as you can from the get-go. CBT teaches people how to accept a personal issue with calmness, which not only helps to make them feel better, but it also puts them in a much better position to make better decisions and use their energy in wiser ways to resolve things.

CBT Utilizes the Socratic Method

Therapists that use CBT need to gain a good understanding of the concerns that their patients have, which is why they are big askers of "why" related questions. They encourage those they help in asking themselves questions to clear up thoughts.

CBT Uses a Directive and Structured Approach

CBT therapists set agendas for their sessions with patients. They use specific techniques and concepts that are taught to people during each session. CBT is a method that focuses mainly on the goals of the patient. Therapists never tell people what their goals ought to be and what they should be able to tolerate. They use a directive sense of showing them how to think and act in ways to better obtain what they desire. They never tell people *what* to do, but instead *how* to do it.

CBT is based on an Educational Model

CBT is, thankfully, one of the best therapeutic methods thanks to the fact that it is supported by science and the reactions of emotion and behavior that are studied. The goal of CBT is to assist patients in *unlearning* unwanted reactions and learn new, more positive ways of acting.

CBT is a method that didn't just evolved around talking, but with the benefit of learning how to act in a more positive manner as well. It yields greater and faster results for patients that undergo this sort of therapy since they ultimately learn a life-long skill.

The Theory of CBT Relies on the Inductive Method

Rational thinking is based upon facts. Many times, we naturally upset ourselves about things especially when a situation doesn't turn out the way we imagined it to be. Think about how much time you could save from being upset if we all realized this.

The inductive method encourages people to look deeper at our thoughts as if they were hypotheses that can be later questioned and tested. When we find out that our guesses are not correct after receiving new intel, we can then change our trail of thought to be in line with how a situation realistically is.

The Techniques and Theory of CBT Rely On the Inductive Method

Think back to when you learned multiplication tables. If you tried to learn them by spending just an hour a week studying, you probably are still wondering what 5 times 5 is equal to. When you were younger, you likely spent many hours at home studying these tables, more likely with flashcards, right?

The same concept can be applied to psychotherapy. When goal achievement is obtained, it can take a long while if you were to only think about the topics and techniques taught to you for an hour per week.

Cognitive behavioral therapists assign weekly projects for their patients to work on. This encourages them to practice the techniques they have acquired and use them in real-life situations, ultimately changing their frame of mind more positively.

How Cognitive Behavioral Therapy Works

As you have learned from the previous chapter, cognitive behavioral therapy, or CBT, is a psychotherapeutic treatment method that assists patients in truly grasping their thoughts and feelings, why they feel a particular way, and what influences the way they feel. This type of therapy is most commonly used to treat a range of disorders such as anxiety, depression, phobias, and addictions.

Cognitive behavioral therapy is a short-term treatment that hones in on assisting patients to conquer specific issues. During CBT treatment, patients learn how to see as well as change disturbing thought processes and destructive behavioral patterns that lead to negative emotions and behaviors.

The fundamentals of the cognitive model

A large portion of cognitive behavioral therapy and its ability to truly work for patients is in its way of cognition, or the way we think about things and what the content of our thoughts are and how they are conceptualized.

There are three main levels of cognition:

1. Core beliefs

2. Dysfunctional assumptions

3. Negative automatic thoughts

CBT Background

Cognitive behavioral therapy was modeled more than 40 years ago to help in the treatment of depression. It is not an effective behavioral model in treating panic disorders, PTSD, anxiety, phobias, insomnia, marital conflicts, substance abuse, bipolar disorder, and many other negative ailments/issues people face.

CBT has been recently shown to have a greater effect on the mind than even prescription medications do, especially in the treatment of insomnia. *CBT relies on its need to identify, challenge, and ultimately change how situations are viewed.*

The way we think is like wearing a pair of glasses that have the power to make us see the entire world in a particular light. This type of therapy heightens our awareness of how we perceive things and how our reality determines how we think and behave.

How CBT Works

The entire purpose of cognitive behavioral therapy is to switch around our way of thinking and the behaviors associated with our thought processes. This method of therapy helps many people solve emotional, social, medical and work related issues by diving into the past to help provide clearer insight into our feelings and why we think and feel the way we do. CBT targets our thoughts and beliefs that we feel right now.

There are specific skills that are involved when recognizing and fixing distorted thinking, modifying beliefs, and how to relate to others in an entirely new way, which helps patients learn to behave in ways that are more desirable.

The fact is that negative cognitive perceptions will lead one to unhealthy thoughts and behaviors. When one experiences something stressful, automatic and intrusive thoughts come to mind that greatly affect their moods and emotions of the situation. This can cause someone to overact, feel sick, or fret. This is because they are making false assumptions on the meaning of things they experience based on an unreliable truth.

For instance, someone who fears going to the dentist may dwell on the pain they felt from a previous possible dental procedure. This fear is likely triggered by a childhood traumatic event. This can cause them to lose sleep, deal with anxiety, and neglect caring for their teeth altogether.

Interventions Practiced with CBT:

- Avoid generalizations and all-or-nothing thinking

- Challenge underlying assumptions

- Correct thinking so that it more closely resembles reality

- Describe, accept, and understand rather than judge.

- Develop awareness of automatic thoughts

- Distinguish between rational and irrational conclusions

- Enhance awareness of mood

- Examine the validity and usefulness of a particular thought

- Focus on how things are rather than how they should be

- Gradually increase exposure to things that are feared

- Identify and modify distorted beliefs

- Identify problem areas

- Identify what is realistic; is what you think really true?

- Keep a cognitive behavioral diary

- See a situation from different perspectives

- Stop "mind reading" and "fortune telling" practices

- Stop catastrophizing (thinking the worst)

- Stop negative thinking

- Stop personalizing and taking the blame

  - Test perceptions against reality

Part 2: Identifying Problems in Your Life

The Basics of Anxiety and Depression

What is Anxiety?

By definition, anxiety is *a feeling of worry, nervousness, or unease, typically about an imminent event or something with an uncertain outcome*. Anxiety involves a physiological state of mind that is labeled by behavioral, emotional, somatic, and cognitive components. When combined, these aspects create feelings of apprehension, worry, and fear, all tell-tale signs of anxiety rearing its ugly head.

If that wasn't enough, anxiety is commonly accompanied with physical ailments such as chest pain, nausea, shortness of breath, headaches, stomachaches and palpitations of the heart.

Every single one of us deals with anxiety, whether it's from overwhelmingly large corporate presentations, or getting in front of an audience, or meeting the in-laws, life is inevitably filled with moments that will lead to anxious thoughts and feelings.

Unfortunately, unless you have supernatural powers to see into the future, you live each day, not truly knowing the repercussions that today's actions can have on tomorrow.

Anxiety is a bodily reaction to unfamiliar or dangerous environments and scenarios that we are naturally given at birth. Everyone has the tendency to get anxious from time to time and feel distressed or uneasy. Feeling anxious from time to time is completely normal, for it gives us the boost we need to be consciously aware and alert to prepare us for certain situations. Our body's "fight-or-flight" response is under this umbrella of reactions.

Our bodies are naturally equipped to prepare ourselves to deal with possible threats, which are why our heart rate and blood pressure increase, we sweat, and our digestive systems are inhibited.

Imagine feeling as if your heart was going to jump out of your throat every waking moment of your life, even during the calmest of moments. Picture a life where you have issues concentrating on everyday tasks, where you may be frightened to leave the safety of your home when you cannot fall or stay asleep because your mind is in a constant whirlwind of thought. Living with an anxiety disorder is debilitating and can lead to other negative outcomes, both mentally and physically.

Potential Causes of Anxiety

All human beings are unique, which makes common disorders resonate differently from one person to the next. Several factors cause anxiety disorders to plant themselves in our mind and grow. Some influences may be:

- Chemistry of the brain
- Life events
- How we grew up
- Environmental factors
- Genetics

The factors listed above are the basics that lay the groundwork to potentially be a victim of anxiety, but those below mixed with any of those above could set one up to be someone that is at a higher risk than others in the development of an anxiety disorder:

- Alcohol, prescription medication or drug abuse
- Chemical imbalances in the body and/or brain
- History of anxiety that runs in family bloodlines
- The occurrence of other mental health issues

- Physical, emotional or mental trauma

- Side effects one has to medications

- Stress that lasts an extended amount of time

The feelings and thoughts that anxiety creates can easily make anyone feel alone. Ironically, anxiety and all the baggage that comes along with it is one of the most common of mental illnesses in the U.S, with over 40 million American adults living with one of these disorders every day.

When it comes down to living with an anxiety disorder, you must recognize what symptoms worry you and find ways to relieve yourself of them. This is much easier said than done. Some people never really know what triggers their anxiety, while others can pinpoint certain things and avoid them at all costs. Triggers can be almost anything and are fueled by specific events that have happened in the past or are set off by a combination of different things.

Some types of triggers are set off by:

- Illness

- Physical or emotional distress

- Relationships and/or friendships

- School-related stress

- Stressful situations

- Ways you process things happening in your life

- Work-related stress

For some, anxiety attacks appear out of nowhere and strike when you least expect it at the most inconvenient times. This uncertainty alone can cause one to feel anxious, which is why having the ability to see your triggers before they occur is crucial to one's success to thrive with anxiety.

Having the power to identify what triggers your symptoms of anxiety can not only prepare you for possible scenarios where they are likely to reside but can also help you in developing effective coping skills to deal with your anxiety overall.

Common Anxiety Triggers that We Are Not Well Aware Of

- The hustle and bustle of everyday life. Life is always busy, and there never seems to be time to slow down.

- The inevitable fact that we are only growing older.

- Driving, especially on freeways with many cars or across bridges.

- Not living up to the expectations that we set for ourselves.

- The sense of uncertainty. When we are not in control of situations, we tend to freak out a bit. This comes from lack of communication and anxiety making conclusions for us.

- Ambulance, fire or police sirens.

- Stresses at work – Not performing well enough, not having enough time during the course of the workday to get things done, etc.

- Simply thinking about what triggers your anxiety can be a cause for anxiousness in itself.

- Being too hot is often times directly associated with being claustrophobic.

- The inevitable part of life known as death. This especially goes for individuals who have experienced much loss in their lives.

- Being alone.

- The possibility of finding out that people do not like you as much as you think they do.

- Being judged or verbally attacked.

- Large crowds.

- The inability to predict the future. Those with anxiety often dislike surprises.

- Trying new things.

- Being far away from home or other places familiar to you.

- When many people speak to or at you all at once.

- The struggles that your children may face at school.

- Money! This is a big one. Whether it is saving for a big event such as a wedding or purchasing a home or car, the process of paying monthly bills while still trying to save money for other things is nerve-wrecking.

What is Depression?

Depression is an illness that affects the way we feel, think, and act in negative ways. It causes us to experience periods of sadness as we lose interest in things we love. Depression is a foundation of many other variations of physical and emotional issues that can also further decrease a person's ability to function in their everyday lives.

Depression is often confused with the natural sadness and loss that we feel after a loved one passes, we lose a job, or face difficulties in a relationship. While these individuals may be "depressed" for a certain amount of time, it eventually subsides, and they can get back to normal functioning.

It is important to understand that "being sad" is not the same thing as being plagued with depression. The reason grief and depression are often confused and misinterpreted are because they both involve intense feelings of sadness and withdrawal from normal life activities.

How grief and depression differ:

- Grief comes in painful waves that are mixed with positive memories. Depression involves total mood dysfunction and loss of pleasure in everyday activities for more than two weeks.

- Self-esteem is maintained during grief while in depression, self-loathing and feelings of worthlessness are common.

Depression Risk Factors

Depression has the ability to affect anyone, even those that appear to live in ideal circumstances. Several key factors can play vital roles in the onset of depression, such as:

- *Environmental factors,* such as exposure to violence, abuse, poverty, neglect, etc. These factors make those more vulnerable to developing depression over time.

- *Personality* can even play a role, especially in those with low self-esteem. Anyone that is easily overcome by stresses in life, or those that are naturally pessimistic are all susceptible to depression.

- *Genetics* cause depression to run in family tree. For instance, if one twin develops depression, the other has a 70% chance of experiencing it as well.

- *Biochemistry* causes chemicals in the brain to become out of balance, which can easily cause symptoms of depression to emerge.

Anxiety vs. Depression

Depression and anxiety are two medical conditions that differ greatly from one another. Yet, their causes, symptoms, and how they are treated often overlap. Even though these two mental ailments are discussed frequently, many people have yet to truly understand their differences.

Many of those that suffer from depression also experience frequent periods of "anxious distress" paired with their lowered moods. This leads to feeling restless, tense, and having issues concentrating on daily life activities. It has been found that people who experience this distress induced by anxious feelings along with depression are at a much higher risk of suicide.

Symptoms of major depression:

- depressed mood

- feelings of guilt or worthlessness

- increase or decrease in appetite

- insomnia or hypersomnia
- lack of energy
- lack of interest in enjoyable activities
- slowing of movement
- suicidal thoughts or behaviors
- trouble concentrating

To be diagnosed with depressive disorder, you will have to have experienced at least five symptoms over a two-week span.

Symptoms of generalized anxiety disorder:

- being easily fatigued
- excessive worry
- irritability
- muscle tension
- restlessness
- sleep disturbance

- trouble concentrating

To be diagnosed with an anxiety disorder, you have to have experienced symptoms for at least six months, and they must cause distress in your day-to-day life.

As you can see, there is an overlap when it comes to comparing the list of symptoms of anxiety and depression. However, there are a few very distinct factors when it comes to determining one from the other:

- Those with depression:
    - Move slowly
    - Reactions are dulled
- Those with anxiety:
    - Are more keyed up
    - Struggle to manage their racing thoughts
    - Presence of fear

The Realities of Living with Anxiety and/or Depression

Let's face it, unless you are a true sufferer of anxiety and depression, you do not really know what it is like to live in denial, in fear, in a constant shadow, always second-guessing yourself and those that surround you, to always think of ill thoughts about your future, etc. If you live with or love someone and see the torment of everyday anxiety, you have probably only touched the surface of what they are going through each day of their lives.

Those that live with anxious thoughts and feelings go through panic attacks on a regular basis or have a phobia of some kind and feel ashamed of their "sickness." It has the tendency to make people feel insane, even though they truly aren't.

Naturally, some days are better than others are, but those who experience symptoms caused by these mental ailments typically have a higher count of bad than good days. They often feel that they are always under a dark cloud that pours rain, but that rain is not made up of just water. Those drops from the sky above their head are created from startling visions, disturbing logic, feelings of worthlessness and/or hopelessness, and looks that they receive from both loved ones and strangers when they truly believe they are in a type of personal crisis or feel as if they are about to be pushed over the edge. This is just a small portion of what it is like to live with anxiety.

Learning to Know Yourself Better to Spot Triggers

The many factors that can set off those anxious thoughts and feelings are a bit different for everyone who experiences anxiety. It is important to take time to focus on yourself and learn what things provide you with peace or create tension in your life.

Getting to the Root Causes of Your Anxiety

What many of us do not realize is that many causes that trigger our anxieties to flare up are actually self-produced. While you can blame your situation, family, friends, etc. for you distress, you are the one who perceives life as it goes on around you. The way you view it, analyze, and take it all is all dependent on you. The root reasons behind the curtains of 'Play Anxiety' are usually caused by one of the following reasons.

- **Negative Self-Talk**

Based on the research conducted by behavioral specialists, almost 77% of our thoughts are quite counterproductive and negative. What we don't realize is that we are being our own worst critic and a detriment to ourselves. Learn to become consciously aware of the way you speak to yourself. Write down any sort of negative thoughts for a day and then each day forward practice transforming those negative words or thoughts into a happy, loving one towards yourself. While it may feel weird at first, it will become second nature to you once you practice it for a while. Your self-talk is just as important of a daily habit as any other is.

- **Unrealistic Expectations**

Sometimes, we simply just have too high expectations that create a high world that we struggle to reach. Expecting those to be perfect and remember all details about you is just ridiculous. If your expectations fly way above you, are more than likely missing grand opportunities and are unable to truly recognize the good things that are happening around you which you should be celebrating. This goes for the expectations you have for yourself as well. Are they actually realistic? If not, how can you go about making them more reasonable and achievable?

- **The "Should" Thoughts**

Do you find your brain thinking that you "should do this" and you "should do that" often? Have you ever just taken a moment to actually find the reasoning behind why you "should"? Telling yourself that you should is equivalent to telling yourself that you are not good enough. It leads to negative self-talk fast and ought to be avoided.

38

Make a positive list of the things you should do or become. Are they yours or someone else's expectations?

- **Taking Things Too Personally**

Those with anxiety feel like many things that occur are actually their fault when in reality; it's more likely that it had nothing to do with someone's disgruntled behavior or a glare they received. Learn to not take things too personally because you never know what may be happening in the life of other people. "We are all in the same game, just different levels. Dealing with the same hell, just different devils." If you think you are the cause of someone's actions, speak up, and ask instead of just assuming. This will get rid of many assumptions that negatively feed your anxiety.

Our minds are wired to believe the things that we tell it the most. If we are always engaging in negative self-talk, expect too much of others or ourselves, do things we just merely think we "should" do or worry about those around you, your brain will act negatively as well. It is all about building a positive foundation for your frame of mind for all those thoughts of yours to dwell on. In order to unlock the door to happiness and less stress and/or anxiety, it is time to get thinking in a happy manner!

Methods of Pinpointing Your Anxiety

While you can take all the time in the world to read information about relieving anxiety via the Internet, books or other media, unless you take action and decide that you truly want to make a change to lower your anxiousness, it will never happen. I am an anxiety sufferer and just a couple years back, it engulfed my everyday life and drowned me more than a few times. Over time, I finally came up with a process that assisted me greatly with determining what triggered my anxious thoughts so that I could get a grip on my life and yield them from continuously taking over my personal life.

You can also find anxiety worksheets and books online that have interactive things to think about and fillers that can help you assess what in the world makes you so darn anxious. One of my favorites that I have utilized and recommend can be found at http://www.dr-jane-bolton.com/support-files/finding-anxiety-triggers.pdf. You're welcome!

- **Stop** – When those feeling of anxiousness begin to hit you, stop and take a moment to take a mental note of what you are doing right at that moment. This is easier said than done, for you might be in the middle of a task,

40

conversation, etc. However, it is beneficial to take just a moment to identify when you began to feel anxious.

- **Identify** – Recognizing the onset of anxiety will help you conclude what actually causes it for you personally. If you develop the capability to notice triggers and feelings when they start to dwell, you can put a stop to them faster. Many people don't realize they are feeling anxious until their symptoms are outrageously taking over them. Over time, you will be able to catch on more quickly what is threatening your happiness and overall well-being.

- **Write** – As I become an expert in making mental notes of why you feel anxious, I find that at the end of the day, I write down the events during my day, both the good ones and those that triggered my anxiety. I keep a notepad on my cellular device so that I can quickly access it to jot down notes at the moment and then write them down on paper before heading to bed. Be sure to write down as many details as possible – what you are thinking, experiencing and feeling, etc.

- **Analyze** – At the end of the week is when I choose to review what I have written in my anxiety notebook. You can review it at the end of each day, week, or month, but I do not recommend waiting any longer than that. I wait at least a couple days to a week so that I can see the pattern that my thoughts made. When you are aware of these patterns, you are better able to focus on the causes of anxiety and avoid them.

- **Possibilities** – There are numerous things that you can make the scapegoat when it comes to feeling anxious. If you have adequate knowledge of these ideas, you can review patterns and conquer anxiety. Anxiety in many cases is situational. If you are anxious about being in unfamiliar surroundings, expose yourself to these types of circumstances a little at a time. If your causes are more based on the way you think and view the world, learn to engage in positive self-talk. Once you have a pattern written out, you will be less anxious just by the fact that you have some idea and control over your anxiety situation overall.

Principles of Automatic and Intrusive Thoughts

We, as humans, have between 70,000 to 100,000 thoughts every day that allow us to interpret the world, describe what is occurring and allow us to make sense of our surroundings. We interpret and give things their own meanings without even realizing it. We can decide if things are nasty or pleasant, bad or good, safe or dangerous, etc.

The Science of Automatic Thoughts

Thoughts are electro-chemical impulses that take place in our minds, which means that they are not statements of fact. Cognitive behavioral therapy has shown that it is not events that cause our emotions and reactions, but the meaning that our brains give to these said events and what we think about what is happening itself.

We all can have very different interpretations of the same event, thanks to what we have previously experienced, how we were raised, and our beliefs and values. The meanings we give to events result in how we physically and emotionally feel. When something happens, we naturally notice things, which trigger thoughts that lead to emotions and actions. Here are a few examples:

- The thought: *"I think something bad is going to happen and I will be unable to cope."* This then leads to feelings of anxiety and avoiding/escaping these situations.

- The thought: *"I'm not being treated fairly."* This leads to angry feelings that make us respond by shouting, hitting, etc.

- The thought: *"The world is a dark place."* Similar gloomy thoughts can lead to depression, which can make us isolate ourselves and do less with our lives.

Characteristics of Automatic Thoughts:

- Can be a memory, an image, words, physical sensation, imagined sound or based on our intuition.

- Are very believable; we automatically and naturally believe our own thoughts.

- They just occur, coming into our minds without us even realizing it.

- They are ours, which means they are catered to our lives and our experiences, knowledge, cultures, values, etc.

- Are persistent and become habitual, meaning they repeat themselves over and over. The more this happens, the more believable they become.

The Science of Intrusive Thoughts

Intrusive thoughts are unwanted thoughts that are stuck in our minds and can cause us distress. They pop up from nowhere and cause us a great deal of anxiety. Intrusive thoughts are often focused on violent, sexual, or socially unacceptable images. Many people fear they commit the acts they picture in their minds, which can lead to feelings of obsession and compulsive actions.

The difference between intrusive and automatic thoughts is that intrusive ones are naturally distressing, which can cause negative actions to result from them. Intrusive thoughts are typically about negative things because they are important to us and we tend to pay loads of attention to them.

Intrusive thoughts naturally latch onto things that are priorities to you in life. If you love animals, for instance, you may have a thought that pops into your head of you harming an animal, which can shake your values up tremendously.

45

Yes, intrusive thoughts are normal! What sets everyday people apart from those that struggle with these thoughts is what they decide to do with them. It is when you fail to ignore them and dig deeper that you add 'meat' to these negative thought processes and create a narrative from them in your mind.

Examples of intrusive thoughts:

- Touching someone inappropriately

- The desire to kiss another person

- To hurt someone you care about

- To confess to things you have not done

How to Confront and Conquer Automatic and Intrusive Thoughts

So, how does one go about managing their automatic thoughts and intrusive urges? It is actually very simple; the problem only arises when you pay far too much attention to the urge that comes to mind. If you are very religious, for instance, and you have the urge to shout something obscene during service, ignore this thought.

The more you focus on what pops into your mind, the stronger the urge will become. In other words, the more you give it your attention, the more power you are fueling it with to take control of you.

Learn to label these thoughts as intrusive and remind yourself that they happen automatically. They are not ultimately up to you. When you accept and allow them to happen while not giving them the time of day, you can allow time to pass more positively. Do not engage with the thoughts or actively push them out of your mind, for this is when people become obsessed with them.

Instead, figure out what these thoughts mean to you. Remember, less is more and to give yourself time. Continue with whatever you are doing when these automatic and intrusive thoughts disrupt you.

Understanding the 'Thinking-Feeling-Acting' Connection

Let's relax for a moment, shall we? I want you to clear your mind and imagine the following situation:

You are walking down the street and you see someone you know on the opposite side of the street. You smile big and wave, yet they don't acknowledge you and keep walking. How do you feel?

Well, the way you feel about this situation is going to depend on your thoughts. If you think –

- *"What is the matter? Have I done something to upset them?"*

    o Thinking like this will likely cause you to feel worried or anxious.

- *"Why did they not respond? They must no longer like me..."*

    o Thinking like this will likely cause you to feel saddened.

- *"What is their problem? What is wrong with them?"*

48

- Thinking like this will likely cause you to feel angered.

- *"Oh, I guess they did not notice me."*

  - Thinking like this will likely cause you to feel mildly disappointed.

The ABC Model

The point is, the situations you face every day do not dictate how you ultimately feel, the way that you feel solely depends on the thoughts you have in response to the situation. This relationship is commonly referred to as *The ABC model*.

1. First, at A, we have a situation or **A**ctivating Event. (A)

2. The result is a feeling or **C**onsequence. (C)

3. However, what many of us are unaware of is the thought or **B**elief that links A and C together. (B)

   a. These thoughts are commonly referred to as automatic thoughts, since they arise immediately and automatically. These types of thoughts help to determine the way we feel and just how strongly we feel it.

Let's take a gander back at our example from above again. We started at A with the activating event that led to B, which were the thoughts we had, that led us to C, how we ended up feeling thanks to those thoughts. The automatic thoughts we have can greatly depend on the mood and the way we are feeling at that time. For instance, if you are already feeling anxious, you are more likely to feel anxious when a situation like that of the above arises. Our thoughts and moods are often congruent. Because thoughts and feelings are so strongly connected, it is of great importance to become aware of how outside influences make us feel.

If you are anxious, you will naturally have anxious thoughts. If you are sad, you will become depressed. All these feelings can turn into a vicious cycle that can leave a negative mark on your life and fulfillment. If you are able to notice your thoughts and how they affect your mood, you can have better power on how they affect your future thoughts and actions and eliminate them before they become too out of hand.

Thinking-Feeling-Acting Connection

After connecting our thoughts to the way in which we feel, we can now connect the relationship to this connection to the way we behave and our bodily sensations, since all these elements greatly influence one another.

We start with the situation, which can be either:

- External
    - Things we do
    - Things that happen
- Internal
    - Thought
    - Feeling
    - Bodily sensation

The situation then generates:

- Thoughts
    - Beliefs
    - Images
    - Self-talk
- Feelings
    - What you are internally feeling
    - Your mood

- Your emotions
- Actions
    - What you are doing
    - How you behave
- Bodily sensations
    - Pain
    - Physiological responses
    - Sensations

Let's look at another example:

You are out with a group of people you do not know very well. You are a bit shy and feeling uncomfortable.

- **Thought** – *"I wish I had something interesting to talk about."*
- **Feeling** – Anxious
- **Action** – You try to say something, but since you are anxious, you stumble your words a bit.
- **Body** – You then feel a bit embarrassed, which results in a tight feeling in your chest.

- **Thought** - Then, you think: *"What is wrong with me? I don't even know how to talk to people."*

- **Feeling** – Then you feel sad

- **Body** – You have a feeling of despair in the pit of your stomach

- **Thought** – *"There is no point in even trying anymore."*

- **Action** – You excuse yourself and head home.

When you are home, you begin feeling depressed. You can visibly see that in this type of situation, how your thought processes, feelings, actions, and bodily sensations all play a hand in how you behave.

Part 3: Getting Back Control of Your Life

How to Set Practical and Meaningful Goals

The Importance of Developing Goals

"Begin with the end in mind." – Stephen Covey

Goals play a key role in helping us to move forward in our lives. They are essentially the oxygen that our dreams and aspirations breathe. They are the beginning steps on the adventure we take as well as our last in the path of achieving success. It's vital to truly realize the significance that setting goals have on all our lives.

Goal Setting is Crucial because…

Any planning that you do to prepare and set yourself up for success in the future is a goal. From planning our chores to developing a retirement plan and everything in-between, the small tasks we do every day are helping to set ourselves up for a brighter tomorrow.

Provides Us with Focus

Do you think you could shoot an arrow without a target to hit? If there were nowhere to aim, then you would just be aiming at a random object to strike. Why would you choose to aim at random and what would the purpose behind it be? Exactly.

The bow and arrow example is a literal analogy to how life would be without the existence of goals. Even if you have the potential and drive, without focus, your talent and abilities are useless. Sunlight cannot burn through a magnifying glass without focus, and the same goes for you. You will be unable to ever achieve anything unless you focus on your efforts.

At the end of the day, your goals are what provide you with a direction in your life. When you set goals, you are giving yourself a target to aim at. When you have a clear sense of direction, this allows your mind to hone in on your target. Instead of wasting time and energy aimlessly shooting, this gives you something to actually aim for and hit, a.k.a. reaching your goal.

Provides a Way to Measure Progress

When you set goals, you are then paired with a system to measure your overall progress since you are equipped with a benchmark to compare it to.

For instance, say you have a goal to write a novel that is 300 pages in length. You start to write each day and strive to work hard in doing so. Then, you lose track of how many pages you have written and how many more you must write to reach your quota. Instead of freaking out, you can simply count the pages you have done, determine the progress, and figure out how much you still need to write.

Keeps Us from Becoming Distracted

When you set goals, you are also providing yourself with mental boundaries. When there is an endpoint in mind, you are better at avoiding distractions and remaining focused on the result. This occurs automatically. No matter who or what meets you along the path you are treading to get to your goal, it always stays locked in and insight. This is why successful individuals thrive on setting goals so they can stay automatically locked in and give their goals 100%.

Help Defeat Procrastination

Setting goals creates a kind of personal accountability. Goals have a way of sticking in your mind and if they go uncompleted, they do not just go away. You have probably had that "Shoot, I was supposed to do _____ today!" moment several times in your life. This is your brain's way of reminding you to get back on track. They also help you to overcome laziness.

Give You Motivation

Goals are the root of inspiration and motivation. They are the building blocks to the foundation for your personal drive to complete things in life. When you make a goal, you create an endpoint to aim for and get excited about. It provides you with the sole thought of accomplishing it, which develops the motivation you need to keep up the momentum to get it done.

Goals are tools that give you the energy to focus in a positive direction and are easily molded to fit your priorities when they change. They are able to connect you directly with your innermost desires, which help to motivate you and provide you with something to achieve.

Gives You the Reins of Your Life

The majority of society in today's world is sleepwalking their way through life. Even if they are working hard, they do not ever feel a sense of achievement, which is derived from the fact that they fail to set a sense of direction for themselves.

When you fail to set goals, you are spending your life running up and down endlessly without achieving anything. You are merely just fulfilling the goals of others, not yourself.

Setting goals that are centered on your desires help you to break out of the autopilot many of us are in and genuinely start living consciously. Don't let others inform you of what to do. This is your life that you should be taking charge of in a proactive way. Goals help you to think for yourself and then go out and get what you want.

Gives Us Ultimate Results

All of the most successful people in the world set clear and concise goals, from athletes to business professionals to performers and everyone in-between. When you are able to set goals, then you have the vision to work forward. You are then ensured that pushing yourself will lead you to achieve better results, rather than you just lying around waiting for things to happen.

When actions have the ability to be measured, there is major room for continued improvement. If you fail to specify your targets, you will find that things will never really get better, because there is nothing to work towards, even if you are working your butt off.

When you are setting goals, thinking ahead is the key to create an actionable plan. Even when things do not go according to that plan (and they will, trust me), you then have a system to review and adjust your way to achieve those goals, since you are actually steering toward the vision you have for your life.

Everything we do is created twice: once in the mind, then in the physical world. The mental creation occurs when you set goals and it happens in the real world when you put in the hard work and sweat to bring that goal to life. Without the creation of goals in your mind, the physical representation is unlikely to happen.

Makes Us Have Laser Focus

When your life's purposes has a good sense of direction, your goals then have the power to provide you with the focus you need to know exactly how you should be spending your energy and time.

This energy is the input that is necessary to create any kind of output. When you have a goal, you are able to make a focal point where you can place your energy to be used to make a maximum reward.

Gives Us Accountability

Goals make you accountable. Instead of just talking the talk, you are now obligated to walk the walk. This sense of accountability is essential with you, not anyone else. No one else really knows the goals you create for yourself to accomplish. When you set specific targets, you are better able to stay the course.

The Golden Rules of Goal Setting

Do you know where you will be in five years' time? Do you have a clear objective of what to work on now? Do you know what you wish to accomplish at the end of each day?

As you have already read, goals are the stepping-stones that lead you to a successful life. Without them, you are swimming in a pool lacking in direction and focus. Setting and planning goals give you the power to control your life and the direction it takes, giving you a benchmark in deciphering if you are prosperous or not.

To accomplish goals, you need to know the proper way to set them. You cannot just tell yourself that you want something and expect it to happen. It is a process that begins with a serious consideration of what your desires are and what you wish to achieve. It requires you to work hard.

Thankfully, some steps are easily defined to help transcend the specifics of all your goals. Getting to know each of these steps is essential to your overall success in forming goals that you can accomplish and feel proud of. They are known as the "Five Golden Rules of Goal Setting." Let's dive in, shall we?

1. Create Goals that Motivate

When you set goals for your life, you need to know the importance of motivation and accomplishment. They go hand-in-hand, which means you need to choose goals that are genuinely important to you. This means that they need to hold some sort of value in achieving them. If you don't have very much interest in the outcome of your goals, they become irrelevant and you will not put as much work into them. Motivation is the vital key to accomplishing your goals.

Set goals centered on your high priorities. This gives you the focus that keeps you from creating too many goals. Achieving goals requires commitment. When you feel a sense of urgency to complete them, this maximizes your success levels. When you feel you don't have to complete a goal, you will continue to put it off until the end of time. This will leave you feeling frustrated, which only feeds the unmotivated portions of you. It also fuels the "I am incapable of being successful" mindset.

- *Tip: To ensure your goals motivate you, jot down **why** they are valuable to you. Use this as a value statement to assist you when you begin to doubt yourself.*

2. Set SMART Goals

You probably have heard of SMART goals, but do you apply them to your life? For goals to be powerful, they need to be designed via the SMART application.

- **S**pecific
- **M**easurable
- **A**ttainable
- **R**elevant
- **T**ime Bound

Create goals that are specific

Goals you set need to be well designed. Ones that are generalized will not help you to be successful, since they provide you with no sense of direction. Goals show you the way, so make it easy to get where you want to be by centering them on where you want to be.

Create goals you can measure

When creating specific goals, include dates, amounts, etc. to them so you can measure your amount of success. When you have a way to measure the amount of your success, you will have something to genuinely celebrate when you achieve it.

Create goals that are attainable

Ensure that it's possible to accomplish the goals you set for yourself. If you set goals with little to no hope of achieving them, you are demoralizing yourself right off the bat and eroding your confidence.

This doesn't mean to set goals that are too easy either. When you complete goals that you didn't have to put much work into, it feeds the cycle of non-achievement in the future. Set realistic, but challenging goals. Find the balance. You want goals that require you to raise the bar a bit, for these are the ones that will give you the biggest sense of satisfaction.

Create goals that are relevant

Your goals should be related to the direction you want your life to go. You create a deeper focus when you align your goals with your desires. Setting inconsistent goals is just a waste of your valuable time.

Create goals that are time-bound

All of your goals need to have a deadline of some sort. This gives you a time of when you can celebrate or reassess. Working towards a deadline gives you the sense of urgency you need to achieve your goals faster.

3. Write Goals Down

Physically writing your goals down makes them tangible and real, erasing the need to make the excuse to forget about it. As you jot down your goals, use words like "will" instead of "would like to."

Frame your goal around a positive statement. For instance:

- "I will hold onto employees that exist for the first quarter" instead of "I will reduce the employee turnover rate." The first one is more motivating while the second is just a get-out clause allowing one to succeed.

Tip: Make a to-do list for yourself regarding your goals. When you use a template with your goals on top, then you can view them as the top priority.

Remember to place your written goals in a place that helps remind you every single day what you want to do. Place them on your fridge, mirrors, computer, desk, walls, etc.

4. Create a Plan of Action

This is an often-overlooked step in the process of planning goals. We become so focused on the outcome we desire that we forget to plan all the steps we need to fulfill those desires.

Write down each individual step and cross them off as you accomplish them. This is how you will realize that you are indeed making progress towards the goal. This is important, especially for long-term goals.

5. Stick with It

Setting and planning goals is an activity you will continue to do for the remainder of your life. Do not view it as a means to an end. They are built-in reminders that keep you on track to your ultimate goal and allow you to review them. While your destination may look similar for a long time, you will find that you will always be changing exactly how you get there along the way. Ensure that the necessity, value, and relevance of the goal remain high for you.

Setting goals are so much more than saying you want something to occur. If you continue to live life without clear, defined goals and understand what you truly desire, you have few odds of reaching success. Following the golden rules of goal setting will help you gain the confidence you need to enjoy the satisfaction of achievement that comes with doing what you want to do. What will you accomplish today?

Are Your Goals Really Yours?

If you find yourself constantly reaching for the stars but never quite reaching your goals, you may be surprised to find out that your goals are not actually *yours*. But how? This happens more often than not because we have so many ideas and beliefs that the society embedded into us from the time we first step foot on Earth.

When you are sitting and writing out your goals, you should start by writing them in a flowing manner, not hesitating about what comes to mind. I personally utilize a specific journal for my goals and use post-it notes to identify sections. If you really want to get to the bottom of what your truest desires are, continue writing without distraction.

After you have made your list of potential goals, there are two ways you can dig deeper to determine if they are truly your goals or not.

One way is to look over what you wrote and begin jotting down your own specifics for every goal. This helps you to be specific in what you want and it will either bring you what you ask for or once you have the finer lines figured out, you will find that it is not what you really want. For instance, you want a new car but you fail to determine all the elements, which mean you may get a car that is a total lemon or one that is uncomfortable or stuck with bad gas mileage. This is because you did not list out what you really wanted in that car.

What you find when you list the tiniest of details for each of your written goals is that some will come easily to you, while others will not. This is a good hint that you may want to forego that certain goal. Pay close attention to how easy certain goals and their steps come to you and mark down the ones that you struggle with on a separate piece of paper.

The other way to look and determine goals from your list is to simply go through it once you are finished and cross out any items that you find do not click with you at all. When you crossed certain ones off, you can now work with the ones that remain.

With the goals that remain on your list, you can start to decipher specific elements of each goal. Do you believe that you can achieve that goal? Do you think you should be asking for that? Is it your goal or one from your parents?

When you are able to list everything that is a goal as well as the specifics to achieving it, it is much more likely to be your goal than ones you struggle seeing yourself fit into. If you feel joyous with what you jot down, they are yours. If you are lacking in emotion with others, they are probably not your goals.

Ways You Mess Up Your Goal Planning

Since you have now come to the realization that it may not be your effort holding you back from achievement but rather the goal itself, it's essential to know the ways that people tend to really screw up their goal setting. Here are some ways that people get goal planning all wrong:

- **Setting Goals that are Impractical**

Even if you are feeling fantastic and on top of the world, if you make ambitious goals that lack being realistic, you are only doing yourself more harm than good. It's important to aim high, but ensure your goal is still within reach.

- **Attempting to Do Everything**

When you are focusing on goals that are broad in nature, nothing really is getting the attention it deserves, which leaves you stranded with a road sign with multiple directions. It can be easy to move from one thing to the next with no actual progress. When you are attempting too much at once, you wind up accomplishing nothing whatsoever.

- **Taking to Heart the Thoughts of Others**

It's essential to base all of your goals around your own heart and mind. When you are concerned about what others may think of what you are doing, it can be difficult to find the concentration to focus on achieving your goals. Focusing on the thoughts of others can also make you doubt if your goals are truly yours. Don't let this happen or detour yours from reaching for the stars.

- **Belittling Deadlines**

Effective goals should always be paired up with some sort of timeline so that you are able to hold yourself accountable. The thing is, if you fail to give yourself enough time to do the things required of you, you would find that you seldom, if ever, meet your goals. Don't get too discouraged, but revisit and redo your deadline to make the adjustments needed to achieve success with those goals.

- **Unappreciation of Failure**

Despite trying to avoid it, a vital element of any goal is a failure. If you fail to use the wisdom you gain from your failings, you will find yourself in a rut and always amongst the lose-lose situation. Instead of viewing failure as negative, see it as a way of falling forward, or what I like to refer to it as "failing forward." Failure brings about the chance to begin again but in a more intelligent manner. A failure is just an event, not who you are as a human being.

- **Failure to Review and Assess**

You must schedule times throughout your week to review and assess what you want to achieve and how you are going to go about getting the accomplishment. A review is vital to the goal planning process.

- **Being a Negative Nancy**

Negativity is a wall between you and the possibility of achievement that can also inhibit you from planning positive goals. Bad attitudes should be viewed as a flat tire. You are unable to get very far until you change it. Negativity is a disability that many carry around with them, which inhibit them from being as awesome as they could be.

- **Setting Too Many Goals**

I know, this doesn't seem like a bad thing, right? Well, the thing is, having too many goals in your basket can become a big deal. It can make you set goals that are way too broad and lack focus. When you justify the energy you spend on whatever you have on your table, you will find that you will never quite get to where you want to go. This is the entire reason that having goals is vital in moving forward with anything you do in life. When you make solid goals, it is the first stepping-stone to the path of awesomeness and achieving amazing things!

Goal *Setting* vs. Creating Goal *Systems*

We all want to achieve various things in life, from raising a great family to getting into better shape to leveling up in your career and everything in-between. The path to all those things for the majority of us is all centered on setting specific goals to act upon.

This is how everyone approaches their life's goals. They set them for specific things they want to achieve. But the things is that when it actually comes down to performing the steps to accomplish goals, there is a better way to do this and understand goals. It comes down to the difference between systems and goals.

For instance:

- If you are an entrepreneur, your goal is to create a million-dollar business. Your system is your marketing and sales process.

- If you are a writer, your goal is to write a book. Your system is to create a writing schedule that you follow.

- If you are a coach, your goal is for your team to win the championship. Your system is what your team does in practice every day.

You see the difference there? Now, if you ignored your goals and just focused your energy on a system, would you still receive your desired results? For example, if you were the coach of a basketball team and totally ignored your goal to win the championship and solely focused on what your team does in practice, would you still get results? I certainly think so.

Reasons to Focus on Goal Systems and Not Just Goals

- **Goals Decrease Current Happiness Levels**

When you are working hard towards goal achievement, you are telling yourself you are not good enough yet, but you will be once you achieve that goal.

There is a problem with this mindset. You are teaching yourself to put happiness and success off until you accomplish the next milestone. You are essentially informing yourself you will not be happy or successful until you reach that goal.

This is why you should commit to the process, not just the goal. Picking a goal puts a type of burden on your shoulders where we find unnecessary stress to succeed. When you focus on systems, you can simplify things by focusing on daily tasks and processes.

- **Goals are at Odds with Long-Term Progress**

We are taught to believe that goals will keep us motivated over a long period, but this is more often not at all true.

For instance, picture yourself training for a marathon. People work hard for months to prepare for this type of venture, but once they finish their race, they quit training. Their goal was to finish that marathon and since they have completed it, there is no longer a goal to motivate them. When you focus all of that hard work and energy on specific goals, what is left to push you forward to a further one?

This creates what I like to refer to as the "yo-yo effect," where people go back and forth from working on goals to not working on anything. This cycle is difficult to build yourself up in the long-term. Therefore, you should release yourself from the plague of wanting immediate results. Goal-based mentalities inform you to finish things to reach a goal, so you don't end up feeling like a failure. However, system-based mentalities have no issues moving forward after a goal since it's never about hitting a specific number.

- **Goals Make You Think You Have Control Over Things That You Could Never Have Control Over**

Sadly, we cannot predict the future, at least not yet. Each time we set a goal, however, that is exactly what we are doing. We attempt to plan where we want to be by a certain date and do our best to make it there. We also try to predict how fast we make progress, even though we are unaware of the circumstances that may arise.

This is why building feedback loops are essential for long-term success. They are essential to creating good systems since they allow you to track various pieces without making you feel pressured to predict what might happen. Build a system that signals you when you need to make adjustment instead of trying to make predictions.

Cracking Your Pessimistic and Intrusive Thoughts

I am sure you have heard someone tell you or say, *"Look on the bright side!"* or *"View your glass as half full, not half empty."* I know when I have had these types of things said to me before I embraced a more positive lifestyle, I would typically roll my eyes and heavily sigh as I walked away. However, science is finding more and more evidence that directly links being more optimistic with major benefits on both the mind and body.

Benefits of Positivity on Your Body

Positive thinking alone has a solid variety of health benefits that can drastically change your wellbeing in many favorable ways. Not only does changing your point of view keep your mind in tip-top shape, but also having more focused and positively fueled emotions can help your entire body.

- **Longer life span**

It has been proven that being more optimistic can literally decrease the rate at which you age, which prolongs your lifespan. When you think in a positive light, you are much less likely to die from serious health issues, such as cancer. Pessimism feeds stress, which can make you sick and develop ailments such as heart disease, just to name one.

- **Strengthens your immune system**

If you hate being sick, then positive thinking is not only a much cheaper alternative to over-the-counter medications, but it is a natural remedy that works better than most drugs. If you are a constant Negative Nancy, you are much more likely to get sicknesses like the cold and flu, since negativity weakens essential areas of the brain that help with the immune system's responses.

- **Better able to cope with sickness**

If you do fall ill, being positive helps you to combat that sickness faster and recover from diseases, surgeries, and more. If you are a sufferer of any serious diseases, perhaps, it is time to revamp your treatment with a simple change in mindset.

- **Vibrant health**

With optimism, you are less likely to develop positive-sucking sicknesses such as anxiety and depression, and you are able to change your mindset to not only take care of your body but your mind and overall physical health as well!

Benefits of Positivity on the Mind

- **Combats depression**

Psychologists have found that depression is strongly linked to a negative mindset. When one is able to simply change their point of view to see the positive rather than focus on the pessimistic aspects of what they are going through, they are able to fight against the development of depression as much as 54% more. Positivity improves mood, no matter the situation at hand and is better at treating depression than almost all other therapies.

- **Better able to cope with hardship**

Life inevitably brings us challenges more often than we like, which means, you are bound to face them at some points. When you are a positive thinker, you have a better ability to cope with stresses that arise. This means that even when something looks impossible, you can easily tell yourself to go at it from a different approach to achieve it!

- **Heightened confidence**

Positive thinkers are naturally more confident, meaning they do not want to spend the time pretending they are in the shoes of another person. They want to strive to love themselves the way they are, which naturally boosts confidence levels.

- **More capable to achieve success**

Optimistic individuals are better able to focus on the good they do rather than their failures. They see failures as not shortcomings but as excellent opportunities to learn and grow. They are always open-minded to try out new things and embracing different methods of thinking. This is one of the essential parts of leading a fruitful life.

- **Happier human beings**

Positive people are much more productive and thus live happier, more fulfilled lives. It is all about the law of attraction here. If you think positive, you will then attract positive events in your life! If you are grateful for what you have in life, you will receive more things to become grateful for. So, stop concentrating on your problems and dwell on what you do have and what you have accomplished so far. Better changes will then come to you naturally.

- **More motivated**

Having a positive attitude helps to fuel your motivation levels and help you start on what you wish to achieve. You will find that having an optimistic attitude gets you to where you want to go much faster and easier than dwelling in the negative.

- **Able to notice all the good in life**

There are many people living life at this very moment who are totally oblivious to all that they are truly blessed with. They take for granted multiple things that they should be extremely grateful for. Just as you read a moment ago, you attract what you are. In other words, *"You reap what you sow."*

When you live a life filled with complaining and mourning a "lost destiny" you haven't even tried to fulfill yet, then you go through life with little to no appreciation for the things you already have, which leaves you to risk losing even more. It is a mad cycle if you allow it to happen and continue to feed it.

Being appreciative and grateful can bring your life many good opportunities, so learn to count your blessings instead of being blind to them.

Benefits of Positivity in Relationships

- **Better relationships**

    When you choose to be a more positive-minded individual, you will begin to take notice that the quality of the people you meet change. You will also begin to notice the more positive qualities of those in your life, including strangers you pass by.

    You will ignore their faults, which allows you ample room to start creating meaningful friendships and relationships with a variety of quality folks. An optimistic attitude is much more fun to be around than a pessimistic one.

- **Better first impression**

    When you make having brighter mindset a priority in your everyday life, you will notice that you will naturally attract the same kinds of people. First impressions are important and can help you in developing essential relationships to further your success later in life. View it as building the foundation for future greatness!

Benefits of Positivity on Your Success

- **Ability to create opportunities from problems**

One of the biggest things I realized as I began swapping negativity for optimism in my everyday life was how blind pessimism made me. It literally placed a blindfold over my entire mind. When I embraced positivity, I started seeing my cup half-full, not half empty. I began seeing solutions to problems I would have never solved before, which gave me many opportunities to take and grow from. Despite what you think, all issues can be solved. It is when you take off the blindfold of negativity that you can finally see appropriate solutions.

- **Naturally more resilient**

When faced with an issue, positive thinkers can do whatever it takes to fix the problem and are not hesitant to ask for the assistance of other people. When it comes to extremely negative situations, such as a natural disaster, research has found that having positive emotions encourages groups of people to thrive and provide leverage for one another to ensure survival.

Resilience is something that can be cultivated when you nurture positive thoughts and emotions, especially when it comes to facing terrible events. Positivity plays a huge role in maintaining stress, eliminating depression, and building up the coping skills needed to survive and serve in the future.

Reshaping Your Attitude for a Positive Mindset

As you have learned so far, having a negative attitude towards life keeps us from being happy and affects those that we interact daily with. Science has more than enough proof to show how being positive impacts your levels of happiness and terms of success. This is why making positivity a *habit* with the help of small changes can help you to drastically change your overall life and the mindset you have towards the world.

The life you are living is a direct reflection of your overall attitude. It can be quite easy, almost too easy, to be cynical at the world and see it as a mess of injustice and tragedy, especially thanks to the media that we all spend many hours a day on.

Negativity is holding you back from really enjoying your life and has a great impact on your environment as well. The energy that people bring to the table, including you, is very contagious. One of the best things you can do in your life that is free of charge and simplistic is to offer positive attitude. This is especially beneficial in a world that loves and craves negativity.

One of my favorite quotes of all time comes directly from the King of Pop, Michael Jackson: *"If you want to make the world a better place, take a look at yourself, and make a change."*

As humans, we are creatures of habit. In this chapter, we will outline small but significant changes that can be made to form positive habits that can drastically change the overall mindset of your life around.

Smile

When asked who we think about most of the time, the most honest answer would probably have to be ourselves, right? This is natural, so don't feel guilty! It is good to hold ourselves accountable and take responsibility for ourselves. However, I want to challenge you to put yourself aside for at least one moment per day (I recommend striving for *more*) and make another person smile.

Think about making someone else happy and that warm feeling you get when you receive happiness. We don't realize how intense the impact of making someone smile can have on those around us. In addition, smiling costs nothing and positively works your facial muscles!

Point out solutions, not problems

Embracing positivity doesn't mean you need to avoid issues, but rather, it is learning how to reconstruct the way you criticize. Those that are positive create criticisms with the idea to improve something. If you are just going to point out the issues with people and in situations, then you should learn to place that effort instead into suggesting possible solutions. You will find that pointing out solutions makes everyone feel more positive than pointing out flaws.

Notice the rise, not just the downfall

Many of us are negative just by the simple fact that we dwell too much on the hate and violence that is in our daily media. However, what we fail to notice is those who are rising up, showing compassion, and giving love to others. Those are the stories you should engulf yourself in. When you are able to find modern-day heroes in everyday life, you naturally feel more hopeful, even in tough times.

Just breathe

Our emotions are connected to the way we breathe. Think about a time that you held your breath when you were in deep concentration or when you are upset or anxious. Our breath is dependent on how we feel, which means it also has the power to change our emotions too!

Don't get dragged down by the negativity of others

I'm sure you have gone to work cheerful and excited to take on the day ahead, but then your co-worker ruins that happy-go-lucky mood of yours with their complaints about every little thing, from the weather to other employees, to their weekend, etc.

It is natural to find yourself agreeing with what others are saying, especially if you like to avoid conflict. However, you are initially allowing yourself to drown in *their* pool of negative emotions. Don't fall into this trap.

Conflict may arise, but I challenge you to not validate the complaints of a friend, family member, or co-worker next time they are going about on a complaint-spree. They are less likely to be negative in the future, if they have fewer people to complain to.

Swap have with get

I am sure you often fail to notice how many times we tell ourselves that we *have* to go and do something.

- *"I have to go to work."*

- *"I have to go to the store."*

- *"I have to pay rent."*

- *"I have to mow the lawn."*

You get the picture. However, watch what happens when you swap the word *have* with the word *get*.

- *"I get to go to work."*

- *"I get to go to the store."*

- *"I get to pay rent."*

- *"I get to mow the lawn."*

See the drastic change in attitude there? It goes from needing to fulfill those obligations to be *grateful* that you have those things to do in your life. This means:

- You have a job to go to

- You have enough money to support yourself and your family to provide a healthy meal

- You have a roof over your head

- You have a nice yard

When you make this simple change, you will begin to feel the warmth of happiness snuggle you as the cold blanket of stress falls away.

Describe your life with positive words

The choice of vocabulary we use has much more power over our lives than we realize. How you discuss your life is essential to harnessing positivity since your mind hears what you spew aloud.

When you describe your life as boring, busy, chaotic, and/or mundane, this is exactly how you will continue to perceive it, and it will directly affect both your mental and physical health.

Instead, if you describe your life as involved, lively, familiar, simple, etc., you will begin to see changes in your overall perspective, and you will find more joy in the way you choose to mold your entire life.

Master rejection

You will need to learn to become good at being rejected. The fact of the matter is that rejection is a *skill*. Instead of viewing failed interviews and broken hearts as failures, see them as opportunities for practice to ensure you are ready for what is to come next. Even if you try to avoid it, rejection is inevitable. Don't allow it to harden you from the inside out.

Reframe challenges

Stop picturing your life being scattered with dead-end signs and view all your failings as opportunities to re-direct. There are little to no things in life that we have 100-percent control over. When you let uncontrollable experiences take over your life, you will literally turn into mush.

What you *can* control is the amount of effort you put into things without an ounce of regret doing them! When you are able to have fun taking on challenges, you are embracing adventure and the unknown, which allows you much more room to grow, learn, and *win* in the future.

Write in a gratitude journal

There are bound to be days where just one situation can derail the entire day, whether it is an interaction that is not so pleasant or something that happens the night before, our mind clings to these negative aspects of the day.

I am sure you have read on multiple sites about how keeping a gratitude journal is beneficial. If you are anything like me, I thought this was total rubbish that is until I started *doing it*. I challenged myself to write down at least five things that I was truly grateful for every day. Scientifically, expressing gratitude is linked to happiness and reducing stress.

I challenge *you* to begin jotting down things you appreciate and are grateful for each day. Even on terrible days, there is something to be blessed about!

Becoming Your Own Positivity Hero

If you have ever wondered *how in the world* highly successful people naturally have a knack of see their glass half-full while you struggle to do the same, one of the many keys to success is mastering the art of positive thinking, which is a practice that successful people have. They have a constant positive outlook on life and have positive intentions every day, which allow them to move in their desired direction, quicker.

So, *how* do they do it? In this chapter, we will discuss the practices that help positive people *stay* optimistic, which aids in their overall success!

Daily practice

Believe it or not, those that are more successful truly understand the value of taking care of themselves. They know the impact that running themselves into the ground has on their lives and the work they produce. This means these people are diligent to do what makes them genuinely happy and they go out of their way to ensure they do not over-extend themselves.

Take this tip and start to make it a daily habit to do things for yourself and to further your success in life. Whether it is enrolling in a class or heading to the gym, making time for yourself allows you to reboot and be more motivated and productive.

Absorb inspiring material

Positive people have learned to avoid negative energy and have no tolerance for it. Many people often compare dark and sad things with being negative, which is a wrong concept to have. Some "dark" and "tragic" experiences can be beautiful in a sense.

However, you have the power to decide what "dark" things you allow into your life. Watching people get beaten on television or listening to politicians ramble on and on are not the best things to allow you to absorb. Realize that there is some material out there that is not useful. Those that radiate positivity from their lives know this and spend their time in material that allows them to grow and learn.

Give out compliments

I am sure you have had conversations in your life where you walked away and had the desire to grow those relationships. Another positive aspect of successful people is learning the art of compliments and how to perform the "compliment dance." This means paying compliments and receiving them with grace as well. Genuine compliments bring successful and positive people joy and love sharing their positivity with others.

Surround yourself with positive people

The truth is that negative people *breed* pessimism while positive people obviously create optimism. The more positive people you surround yourself with, the more motivated you will be to take the steps to fulfill your goals and be successful.

See failures as a lesson, not a mistake

Successful people have learned to change their entire mindset when bad things occur in their lives. From small mistakes to substantial failures, they have learned the qualities it takes to pick them back up, dust them off, and see those experiences as a stepping-stone to improving in the future.

If you always view bad experiences as negative, you are just wasting your time and energy that you could be putting into learning and moving forward. View mistakes as a lesson and reframe your mind. View your failures as constant growth.

Avidly play the "appreciation game"

As I have mentioned before, appreciation and gratitude are vital to remaining positive in your life. Throughout your day, be mindful and actively find things that you are appreciative of. As you walk throughout your neighborhood, say to yourself, "I am appreciative of the weather today" or "I am grateful of the awesome conversation that I had with my buddy on the phone."

It may seem weird at first, but once you make it a habit, you will see that being actively appreciative will continuously breed more appreciation, which fuels positive thinking.

The Three Blocks of Producing Better Results

All successful folks are very aware of how much their mindset affects their overall success. Your habitual method of thinking directly affects both your inner and outer world. Your life is an exact reflection of what your mind is thinking. When you change your mindset, you will see major changes in your results.

It's simple; a great mindset equals great results. There are three particular building blocks when it comes to mastering mindset.

- **Absorption**

The information you soak in on a daily basis plays a major role in how your mindset is influenced. The music you hear, the shows you watch, and the websites you scroll through regularly, the books you read, etc. all play a part in affecting your overall mindset.

An important principle that I embrace is what I like to refer to as "GIGO: Garbage In, Garbage Out." The concept is simple. If you choose to absorb trash, the reflection of your life will look like garbage too.

hat you sow is what you reap! If you do not like what you are reaping currently, it is time to perform changes that allow you to reap things you are proud of. That is why, it is so important to be intentional about the things you absorb every single day. Consciously be wise with what you fuel your mind with.

- **Associations**

The people you choose to allow into your life and that you surround yourself with *matters*. If you spend your time with people that empower themselves and you, you will be much more motivated to empower yourself and others.

If you choose to spend your valuable time with unmotivated, insecure, and negatively driven people, you will not be inspired to embrace an optimist mindset and achieve your goals and dreams. If you actively aspire to be a better person, you will find that you will attract similar people. Learn to be consciously intentional with whom you associate your life with.

- **Affirmations**

We talk to ourselves all the time throughout the day. The words you tell yourself help to shape your overall mindset. The inner voice sends messages to your mind that will either help your grow or hinder your progress.

Therefore, reciting positive affirmations is essential to knock down all the barriers you place around yourself. You need to be more aware of what is happening within your mind and learn to take better control over it, instead of letting negativity constantly reside within.

Everything you do counts! From the things you choose to read and watch to the people you choose to associate with, and the conversations you have within yourself. These are the three strongest building blocks to create a better foundation to remain positive, no matter your circumstances. When you choose to pay attention to the things you allow yourself to absorb, you will become a master of the positive mindset.

Recognizing and Modifying Your Core Beliefs

Rediscovering Your Best Self

If you find yourself waking up each day unhappy, it is time to re-evaluate the best parts of your life and revamp your life to once again feel positive. We all get lost in life from time to time. We forget old passions we had, given up interest in pursuit of something else, etc. However, it is never too late to rediscover what makes you great and what makes you feel truly alive.

Recall when you were the happiest

Take a moment to remember when you were the most content with your life. In high school? College? Before marriage, family, and kids? When you began your family? Started your business? Pursued a new hobby?

People peak at various times in their lives and no one peaks at the same time or at the same levels. The key to regaining this again is not to place the good times in a folder labeled 'the past', but to figure out how to get that feeling of contentment back into your life as it currently is. How can you re-incorporate those things that brought you joy in the life you are living now?

Find out what makes you unhappy

Just as important as learning what fuels your positivity, you also need to evaluate the things that make your blood pressure rise and fuel your frustrations too. When you are able to clearly point out the toxic influences, you will be better able to erase them and develop better, healthier ways of living.

We tend to hold onto things from the past that have negative impacts on our current lives. Since it is in the past that is the first reason that it is about time you let it go! No matter what it is, from a toxic ex to a job that drains you, cutting these negative influences will allow you ample space to grow in a positive direction.

Write it out

Thoughts that bounce around our crazy minds can be very overwhelming. We also do not realize the power that our thoughts have over us. They can tell us the things that we do and do not want, as well as what we can and "cannot" do. This is negative and we are the only ones with the power to take action to eliminate these annoying thoughts from inhibiting our success in life.

I have found that organizing thoughts by writing them down makes them more abstract. When you can visualize them on paper, it makes them concrete. Write out a list of pros and cons, random thoughts that pop up, poetry, grocery lists, anything that comes to mind. *All writing can be therapeutic and helps us to rediscover how our voice sounds, which radiates who we truly are.* I challenge you to find yourself again with the power of a good old pen and paper.

Learning to Love Yourself Again

Another essential piece of rediscovering yourself for who you truly are is to learn methods to love yourself again, even after everything you have endured. There are millions of places that offer up 'good advice' to practice self-love, but they never explain exactly *how* to do so.

Loving yourself is a vital piece of the puzzle when it comes to positive personal growth. It allows us to fulfill our dreams and create happy and healthy relationships with others too.

Care about yourself as much as you care about others

This sounds almost too simple, but many of us are not selfish enough when it comes to fulfilling our wants and needs. You are not selfish when it comes to caring for yourself and your wellbeing. Being compassionate to yourself shows concern for you *and* for those in your life as well. You should treat yourself the way you treat your best friend, with care, concern, and gentleness.

Maintain boundaries

Jot down a list of things you need emotionally, what is important to you, and what upsets you. The list can be made up of anything, from wanting sympathy, for being celebrated to being cared for, etc. Whatever is important to you, no matter how silly it sounds, write it down.

The things you write down are what you should consider your personal boundaries. When someone ignores something on that list, you should consider it as them crossing boundaries that you have respectively set for yourself. Do not ignore how you feel if this happens, for they are there to tell you what is right from wrong.

Inform others about the boundaries you have set for yourself and be forthcoming with what you will and will not tolerate. When you are assertive with your boundaries, this plays an important part in building a positive self-esteem and allows you many opportunities to reinforce your beliefs, what you cherish, and what you deserve from life.

Do what you need to in order to be *you*

Take the time to establish the things that make you feel good about yourself and about your life as a whole, no matter what it is. Just learn to be aware of how you feel when you go about acting on certain things. For example:

- Are you exhausted by the work you do, but feel thrilled when gardening?

- Are you joyful when reading aloud to your children?

- Do you feel a sense of fulfillment when you write poetry or volunteer in your community?

Once you figure out what makes you feel good about yourself, make those things a priority by implementing them into your every day or weekly schedule. No matter what, make sure you go out and do them! This may mean you have to give up other things to make time for them, but it also means that you may need to re-evaluate your schedule and life more so that you are doing what you honestly enjoy.

To ensure that you are doing these things, do the things that will get you to those happiness goals such as saving money to buy supplies to paint, waking up an hour earlier, exercising more, etc.

It is important to realize that you need to do what you need to fulfill your happiness goals. You cannot allow yourself to blame others if you do not fulfill these things. It is time to be a little selfish and fill up your own teapot so that you can fill up the cups of others in your life! This will help you to not only feel better and do better by other people, but it will help you to clear the fog on inconsistent negativity from your life and enable you to truly love yourself and your life once more.

Maintaining Positive Mindfulness

As you can imagine, embracing positivity in everyday life can make a profound change in how happy and peaceful your overall life is. When you utilize a positive mindset every day, you will find that life, in general, tends to flow and unfold with more ease and that people in your life then start to respond back to you in more optimistic ways.

I am sure you are aware of this, which is one of the main reasons you are here in the first place! But the real power is behind actually doing it, not just talking and reading about this positive picture. Trust me, I know the struggle of everyday life, and that it can be *a lot* to handle. Even during amazing experiences and opportunities, the chaos and demanding challenges of life seem to overshadow the greatness you do have.

While motivating yourself to maintain positivity every single day is not easy, it is more than possible and certainly worth the effort.

First, positive people are almost always positive, no matter what, because of two key things:

1. They *practice* being optimistic to strengthen this capability further.

2. They *choose* to be positive because it feels a heck of a lot better than drowning in a pool of negativity.

We are not born positive or negative, and one person is not more capable of optimism from the next. Stop making excuses about your skills, challenges, or situations you are enduring when it comes to your level of optimism. There are no aspects that make positivity easy, even though many see it this way.

Positivity is primarily a choice. You need both free will and awareness to succeed and maintain a good sense of optimism in your life. Guess what? Every person, even *you,* is wired with free will and conscious awareness! You are always in a good place to be more positive and start reaping the benefits from it.

When you are aware of yourself and your life, you will then notice when you are starting to venture down the path of negativity. Having this awareness jumpstarts the choice between optimism and pessimism. Below are some awesome tips you can begin to practice to gain optimum results!

Ways to Be Happier Daily

Practice the Power of Positive Thinking

The power behind positive thinking is undeniable. When you think positively:

- You receive better results. When you love the new evidence of improvement, you strive further to continuously achieve it

- You better notice your flow of behaviors and choices. You are better inclined since you know how you are feeling and thinking.

- You create better results and others in your life respond in favor.

- You feel more at ease.

- You behave in a more optimistic manner thanks to the elimination of the negative cloud raining over you daily.

- You have less time for negativity when embracing optimism.

- You allow your mind to be fueled with more positivity, which has amazing effects on your physical, mental, and emotional health.

- You are better able to recite positive statements to yourself.

- You actively choose to utilize the power of positive thinking each day.

When Faced With a Challenge, Choose Positive Responses

Problems are inevitable and will arise. It is just a part of life. We all face them, but it is critical to our overall wellbeing *how* we interact with issues. When you negatively react, you end up majorly draining your energy and affecting your health in bad ways.

Positively facing challenges at hand does not necessarily mean you are forced to be happy about them. It is about learning to choose the best perspective in all situations. We all have a choice of what type of perspective we choose, which in return, affect how we feel.

Here are ways to embrace positivity no matter the scenario(s) you are faced with:

- Instead of locking in your first negative thought, ask yourself these questions instead:

    o What is the situation teaching me?

    o What is a positive, more peaceful way I can interpret and approach this situation?

- Take a moment to breathe and count to 10 (sounds too simple but work *wonders.*)

- Take notice of how you are feeling and thinking.

- Realize that you have the ability to pick your perspective and nothing can make you think anything. Remember that your mind is a sacred place that is *yours.*

Practice self-love

The bulk of all positivity and the greatness that comes with it begin with you. It has little to do with what is happening in your life and everything to do with whatever is happening within yourself. When you feel good about yourself, it is much easier to jump on the path of positivity.

If you don't believe or love yourself, you are bound to face numerous challenges when it comes to generating a positive attitude that is required for success in life. To help create a better relationship with yourself, you need:

- to do something at least one time per week that is an act of self-care. Think about any action you take to make yourself feel nurtured and supported. Even think about things you do for others or that you do for those you deeply love and start doing similar things for yourself!

- to practice the act of forgiving yourself instead of beating yourself up about weaknesses, goals that are unmet, regret, mistakes, the past, or guilt.

- to take stock of the things you do love about yourself. Anything from skills, achievements, triumphs, strengths, etc. Learn to love the journey you have been on so far.

Daily Actionable Steps for Positivity

I became aware of the power that a positive, habitual routine played in my life once I honestly started to embrace and utilize it. Here a few things I personally use in my daily positivity routine, plus some others that people find helpful in their day-to-day lives to radiate optimism:

- Regular exercise

- Planning out your day

- Listening to uplifting music that plays a part in motivating and inspiring you

- Praying or having a conscious conversation with life and the universe

- Gratitude

- Visualization practices

- Meditation routines

- Listening and speaking positive affirmations out loud

- "Thought Interruption Technique"

    o Jot down recurring negative thoughts

    o Write out an alternative thought for each one

    o When you are aware of negative thoughts, practice interrupting them and instead, recite the positive thought to take its place

    o Repeat those positive thoughts until it becomes familiar to you

- Choose to end every day on a positive note so that you are able to capture quality sleep.

- Celebrate every achievement

- Give thanks and learn to be blessed with what you do have in life

- Repeat affirmations that help you feel better about yourself

- Listen to guided meditations

- Journal things that inspire you and motivate you to live a more positive lifestyle

Ways to Have Happier Thoughts All Day, Every Day

If you learn the power of harnessing positive thinking, you are more likely to attract positive circumstances in life. The same goes for negativity. The more pessimistic you are the more negative situations will arise. The blessings you receive in your lifetime are ultimately up to you. If you think and act positively, you will then unknowingly call positive things to appear. If you are pessimistic and cynical, you will always be caught up in a whirlwind of negatively self-inflicted prophecies.

Like attracts like!

Meditation

I was skeptical about meditation at first, but once I started utilizing it in my everyday routine, that skepticism quickly faded. It has been one of the best and one of my favorite methods of removing negative emotions from my life and recovering with a nice dose of positive emotions and spirituality.

Meditation works to rejuvenate your mind, which makes it much more resilient when negativity does arise in your life. It not only rids us of all those bad chemicals, stress, and anxiety in a physical way but in an emotional sense as well.

I like to explain meditation to my readers like this: If you are wired to always be miserable, meditation should be viewed as a big RESET button that allows you to unplug, turn off, and tune out. Meditation is a practice that can be easily learned and implemented so that when you turn your brain back on, it is now using frequencies of positive thinking instead! Pretty cool, right?

If you use meditation often and long enough, you will discover that a lot of the damage that negativity has caused becomes eliminated and you are left with a nice, clean slate to paint all on your own with your new positive mindset.

Be Thankful

Gratitude, no matter in what context, always has the power to instill more happiness in our lives. In fact, scientifically, it gives our brains a big dose of dopamine, which is a 'feel-good' chemical that erases negative emotions and thoughts.

Gratitude is an action that conjures the law of attraction we have discussed previously in this book. If you make an honest effort to be grateful, you will find that you end up being blessed with more! Make sure to write in that gratitude journal every single day. I like to do so right before I hit the hay. (That rhymed!)

Be Kind

Kindness is another proven action that washes the stress away and leaves us feeling joyful and content with our lives. Kindness is *contagious* within the human race. When a person is kind to you, you feel motivated and very inspired to pay it forward, right? That is how much power it holds!

Kindness is also an action that helps to influence gratitude as well since it makes us more inclined to be truly blessed.

Stress-Less

If only life were 'stress-less', right? Since this will never be the case unless you live in a hole and never come out for sunshine, you need to learn how to extinguish the flames of stress and all of the unhealthy things that come with it such as anxiety, depression, and addiction, to just name a few.

Stress is caused by dwelling on the things that are going wrong in our life. Stress is often classified as 'emotional distress', which, believe it or not, is self-inflicted. If you work too hard, you will start to become unhealthy. If you do not sleep enough, you will become exhausted. If you neglect your friends and family, you will develop loneliness. So, how does one *win*?

You must rid yourself of life's negativity and choose to *relax*. This means take care of yourself, both inside and out. Drink lots of water, eat right, exercise, meditate, get enough sleep, etc. Learn to never bite off more than you can consume. When you practice self-care, you will start to feel stress fall away from you.

Be Your Biggest Fan

Tell yourself *at least once per day* how talented you are, how gorgeous you are, and that you are just plain *AWESOME*. When you do this every day and make it part of your routine, you will start to truly believe it. Pep talks work folks. They uplift, inspire, and motivate you to make the best in your life every single day.

The next time your gut feeling informs you that something is wrong, instead of saying to yourself, "*This is bad*," affirm yourself that you can handle whatever life throws your way and tell yourself, "*I will be okay.*"

Pulling Positivity from the Rubble

There will be times in your life that it feels like the entire world is against you even though you are doing everything to stay above water. It may be a reason why you are still reading this book. In chaotic situations, it can be difficult to remain positive, which may incline us to act out in negative ways. Well, you see what good that does, none. This will only attract more negativity to your life and at the end of the day, no one wins this game.

If anything, negative situations are calling out in dire need for you to stay positive and ride out the tides of bad situations. There are ways to stay positive that I have learned to use, especially when it seems like life is crumbling around me.

Ways to Easily Optimize Positivity in Negative Situations

- Know that it is not possible to please everyone in your life. No one has the power to do this, no matter how hard they try. You need to realize that you will have to let certain people go throughout your life to relieve negative burdens.

- View negative situations you are in as "training sessions" that will help you to succeed later in life. The higher you climb, the worse situations can get. These scenarios are preparing you for future endeavors.

- Have favorite motivational and/or inspiring quotes either memorized where you can recite them to yourself or placed where you can easily see them every day.

- Talk to someone that is a positive influence in your life to help encourage you to keep trucking forward.

- Learn to openly admit to the mistakes you make. Remember, you are human and no one in this world is perfect.

- One of my favorite quotes to remember regarding mistakes: *"A life spent making mistakes is not only more honorable but more useful than a life spent doing nothing."*

- Holding onto negative feelings and emotions will do more harm than good. There is no good reason for you to grasp pessimistic points of view.

- Learn to maintain a positive point of view of those in your life. Even if you do not like their behavior or the message they are sending, it doesn't mean you should hate them personally. This hate only makes you harbor a dark negativity that is hard to shake.

- If you come across negativity in people or messages, learn to ignore, and avoid them. They are a waste of your valuable time.

- What do people say about you? View the content in a positive light so that you can act upon it and improve yourself. Don't avoid and reject messages people are trying to get to you.

- Learn the power of speaking in a gentler tone to help reduce tension in situations.

- Take a nice, deep breath to calm yourself down when the going gets rough so you are able to think clearer and in a more positive manner.

- Don't respond when you are angry. If you are not sure if you are calmed down, do not respond to something until you know you are.

The Five Rules of Positivity in Negative Situations

In situations that are hard to keep up a positive persona, it is even more essential to stay positive so those around you do not judge you by your inability to handle situations that arise. Negativity only tends to make things worse, which later fill you with more resentment, anger, disappointment, and later guilt. No one has time for this.

The tried and *true* way to beat negative situations is to keep and maintain an optimistic attitude. This is a choice you must make, especially when seeing difficult scenarios as learning curves instead of a huge pothole in your road to success. Here are the five rules of staying positive when life gets hectic.

Rule 1: You are in control of how you respond

You and only you can control your response to situations. Take a deep breaths, count to 10, and do whatever you can to remove yourself from the negativity that tries to overrule your behavior. When you are calm, you are more able to think clearly about how to solve things.

Responding in correspondence to how you are feeling will only make the situation worse than it already is. *"If you cannot say anything nice, then don't say anything at all."* A good rule of thumb to adhere to!

Rule 2: Learn from negative situations

It is easier said than done, but viewing pessimistic scenarios as opportunities to grow and learn help you to find opportunities in difficulty. Instead of using your energy to react negatively, do something positive to help make the situation at hand better.

Rule 3: Admit mistakes

As a society, we tend to forget that we are human and are allowed to make mistakes. We all have shortcomings. But one thing we can do to make situations better is to admit our mistakes instead of trying to deny them. Learn from the mistake you made that developed the bad situation, learn from it and move forward.

Rule 4: Maintain a positive point of view

In negative situations, our opinions have a funny way of becoming jaded. This is when remaining positive is essential so that we do not allow ourselves to jump to conclusions. When you become proactive in dealing with the adversity of certain circumstances, you can help to affirm yourself and your positivity.

This is especially important when we are forced to work under pressure. It can be difficult to keep up a positive attitude, but this is where positivity plays a key role in developing a good or bad outcome from a situation.

Rule 5: Highlight the Positive

- Don't go back and forth between negative and positive emotions. When negativity comes to the surface of your mind, flip back to an optimistic point of view and remain there.

- Make the positive truths concrete by being true to yourself and your life's work.

- Discard all negative thoughts that are born from pessimistic situations. There is nothing good to be gained from acting out in a bad way.

- Affirm your attitude with your words and actions, not just one or the other.

Easy Ways to Live a More Positively Driven Life

To reduce anxiety, one must be willing to put in the work to make positive changes and better ways of thinking a habit. There are many small changes one can make that can potentially have significant positive results in their life. This chapter is full of just a few of the best ones!

Mindful Moving

We are a species that tends to live in the future. Everything we do in the present moment is aimed towards a potentially better outlook in the long run. We forget to take the time to enjoy and live in the present. When you spend more quality time at the moment, it is much easier to be positive and has realistic expectations. If you spend all your time in the future, you are just setting yourself up to be a major worry-wart. Move slowly during your morning routine, and the rest of your day will hopefully be followed by the same action.

Start Off Your Day Positively

The method in which you start off the day from the very beginning sets the tone for the remainder of it. This is why it's so often stressed to get up a bit earlier so you can perform your morning routine at your own pace. We often are functioning at full speed and are susceptible to getting lost in stress and the loss of power we have over our lives.

Add Value to another Life

The vibes we send out into the world daily have a funny way of coming back to hug us or kick us right in the butt. What you give is typically what you receive.

- **Help out** – Lend a hand to a friend when they need it, give someone a ride or ask someone if they need assistance.

- **Listen** – Learn how to listen instead of talking over people. Most times, people just need a listening ear that is non-judging and attentive to what they are saying.

- **Boost moods** – Give hugs (when appropriate), smile at people while making eye contact. Play feel-good tunes when hanging out with friends or suggest an inspiring movie. Encourage those going through tough times.

Don't Let Fear Overrule Your Life

There will be times you want to take life by the horns, be risky, and take a chance. But anxiety has a way of pulling you back from these opportunities. We tend to spew out vague fears to make excuses for not taking chances. We are fueled by fear instead of what is possible if we try. Ask yourself what is the worst that could happen. This will make way into figuring out how to spend time in unfamiliar situations that could lead to potentially bigger turnarounds.

Find Your Happy Place

Turns out that finding your happy place is a real thing and is especially recommended for those that experience periods of anxiousness. Mentally relocating ourselves when our anxiousness flares up is a great way to remain relaxed, calm, and in the moment. It gives us the freedom to lose ourselves in a moment. Happiness is a state of mind. The more you practice getting there, the easier it will become for you.

- Recall places that you have been that you have liked for their sights or sounds.

- Use the method of imagery or visualization to bring about that place you seek.

- Ensure that you choose a place that you experience happy emotions.

- Try to recall where you were when those feelings of deep meaning and/or contentment engulfed you.

- Maintain open-mindedness

Write

I know that writing has helped me time and time again when it comes to my feelings of anxiety. Whenever I was feeling particularly anxious or in some type of emotional turmoil, I would grab a notebook, my phone or my laptop and jot out my feelings. To do this effectively, let go your fear of judgment. Unless you give your journal or whatever you write on to someone else to read, this is just for you to vent. It also puts a positive spin on being an anxiety sufferer.

I have created many great reads, such as short stories and poems, from what I was feeling at a certain moment. Do not think of writing as attempting to avoid anxiety. You are living in that moment by not only documenting it but over thinking about it in a constructive manner. Seriously, try it. I assure you that you will feel much better about it. Plus, if you write often enough, you may see a pattern in your life that you wish to or need to change.

Find the Optimism within Negative Circumstances

I have found that one of the most effective ways to create a positive point of view on any kind of situation is to ask more helpful questions. What is good about the situation? What is a new opportunity that might be lying within it? Thinking like this has a much more positive effect on my life than asking what I did to deserve this, etc. Do not rush these inquiries though. Take time to process your feelings and thoughts towards a situation. Trying to force positivity while in emotional turmoil usually isn't very effective.

Cultivate a Positive Environment

The more time you spend from outside media such as television, magazines or the World Wide Web, the better. It is essential to have positive influences in your life to lead your life in such a way. Ask yourself what some negative influences in your life might be and what sources of information lead to negative thoughts. When going through your answers to these inquiries, think about how you could spend less time around these things. You now have a lot more time free to do things that will make positive impacts on your life!

Be Comfortable in Your Own Skin

This one can be a challenge, especially for those who suffer from anxiety. We fear judgment and try to be perfect when in reality; no one on this planet can achieve perfectionism. Learn to accept who you are and the body in which you were born in. If you are constantly wishing to change things about yourself that are impossible to change, you will never be happy with yourself. It kills any potential to be happy. When you are not comfortable in your own skin, this leads to problems with confidence, self-esteem, and your overall well-being. Distance yourself from people who make you feel less than happy.

Appreciate What You Have

If you are always seeking for what others have and what you don't, you will always picture your life as the grass is greener in other people's yards and not appreciate and become grateful for all the wonderful things you have in your life already! You will feel constantly miserable and as if something is missing. This is the same for comparing yourself to others as well. While it may set a certain benchmark to achieve success, comparing yourself with others does become unhealthy at some point.

Make sure your motives are aimed towards prosperity. Simply learn to appreciate what you have and take time to acknowledge that everyone is fighting their own battles. You would be surprised by just how many people wish they had *your* life.

Let Go of Anger and Resentment

Resentment towards other people is only going to poison you to the core. We hang on to anger with the assumption that the person will eventually realize what they did wrong. But, we are only hurting ourselves. Learn to let go and forgive, no matter how long the process takes.

Live with an Open Mind

Those who are narrow-minded are only hurting themselves. You will feel agitated more so than those that live openly because of how firmly you stand in beliefs that many others may not live by or approve of. If you learn to live your life as your own and respect that others are more than capable of living theirs as is, you will be happier overall.

Listen to Music that Reflects the Mood that you wish to be in

There are plenty of studies to show what impact music has on our brains. If you want to be in an upbeat mood, turn up your positive music! It is a sure-fire way to brighten your day. Share it with those around you! I know, for me personally, getting out and driving for a bit with my music blared with some of my favorites, upbeat tunes help my anxiety out immensely.

Other Ways to Live More Positively

- Wake up with the strongly held belief that today will be a great day.

- Inform those that you love that you care about them and their well-being.

- Unhappy? Only you have the power to change your life.

- Things will not always be bad, tough or rough. Things will get better.

- Make a list of the things going right in your life instead of dwelling on all the things going wrong.

- Engulf yourself in your favorite activity or hobby if you are stressed. Anything that boosts your mood is approved!

- Even when things do not go your way or happen unexpectedly, learn to view things as positive mishaps.

- Learn to be easy on yourself. Do not always strive for perfection.

- Enjoy nature or other places that help you escape from reality for a bit. This can be soothing and help automatically relieve anxiety symptoms.

- Turn up your favorite song. It is a sure-fire and quick way to perk up!

- Balance your time wisely between work, school, relationships, and yourself.

- Each day is a gift. Treat it as such.

- Research has shown that those who are optimistic tend to live longer!

- Unplug and take breaks from social media, schoolwork, and workplace projects. Everyone needs and deserves a break sometimes.

- Eat things that nourish your body. A healthy vessel gives way for more positive energies to be felt throughout the day.

- What are you passionate about? Learn to become a master at whatever drives you.

- Adequate sleep, rest, food, and exercise all play roles in a healthy lifestyle and mind.

- Laugh often and smile as much as you can!

Dealing with Negativity: Fear, Worry, Anxiety, Procrastination, etc.

Methods to Control Emotions

Emotions are natural in human nature and are very present in pressing and painful times. Every day, we are driven by some force of emotions:

- We take chances because we get excited about new opportunities

- We cry because we are hurting and make sacrifices for those we love

Those are just a couple examples of emotions. They dictate our actions, intentions, and thoughts with authority to our rational minds. Emotions can become a real problem, however, when we act too fast or we act on wrong types of emotions, which cause us to make rash decisions.

Negative emotions, such as bitterness, envy, or rage, are the ones that tend to spiral out of control the most, especially when triggered. It only takes one slip of our emotions to totally screw up the relationships in our lives.

If you have issues controlling your emotions, here are some steps that you can implement in your everyday life that will help you regain rationality, no matter what challenging situation you are facing:

Don't react right away

You are more likely to make mistakes when you react right away to emotional triggers. When reacting right away to these triggers, you are likely to say and do things that you will later regret.

Before acting on emotions, take a deep breath to stabilize your impulses. Breathe deeply for just a couple minutes and you will be able to feel your heart rate return to normal. Once you become calmer, remind yourself that feeling this way is just temporary.

Find healthy outlets

Once you have managed your emotions, you need to learn how to release that buildup in the healthiest way possible. Emotions are something that you should never be bottled up. Talk to someone you trust. Hearing their opinion of the matter can help to broaden your thoughts and regain control.

Many people keep a journal to write down how they feel. Others engage in exercise to discharge their emotions. Others meditate in order to return to their tranquil state. Whatever activity suits you, find it and use it when emotions get high.

Look at the bigger picture

All happenings, both bad and good, serve a purpose in our lives. Being able to see past the moment strengthens your wisdom. You may not understand certain circumstances right away, but over time, you will see the bigger picture as the pieces of the puzzle fall into order. Even when in an emotionally upsetting time, trust that there is a reason that you will comprehend in time.

Replace your thoughts

Negatively fueled emotions create negative recurring thoughts that create cycles of negative patterns over time. When confronted with these emotions, force them out of your mind and replace them with more positive thoughts. Visualize the ideal ending playing out or think about someone or something that makes you happy.

Forgive your triggers

Triggers could be the ones you love the most like your best friend(s), your family, yourself, etc. There will be times that you may feel a sudden wave of rage when people do things that annoy you or a self-loathing feeling when you remember back in the past when you could have done things differently. The key to managing your emotions is to first, forgive. This allows you to detach from your jealousy, fury, and resentment. As you forgive, you will discover that disassociating yourself from these feelings will do you a world of good.

Every day, we are constantly reminded of how strong and prominent our emotions are and the power they have. We are bound to take the wrong action from time to time and feel the wrong things. To avoid acting out, simply take a few steps back and calm your spirit that is heightened from outside forces.

Beating Procrastination

Procrastination is truly an art of putting off what we could do today for tomorrow. It is also the bane of anxiety sufferers everywhere. This chapter outlines some tried and true ways to overcome procrastination and perhaps even some of the pesky anxiety symptoms as well!

Do what scares you!

- **Dive in** – This method is simple by just doing something, even if it scares you. You must plunge right in and do it without giving yourself time to think too much about it. It may not always be pretty, but it works 99% of the time in getting things done.

- **Inch towards it** – If forcing you to do it doesn't do the trick, try deception. Instead of writing about procrastination, for example, write how much you hate writing at first. While this sounds counterproductive, it is a great trick to get you into the swing of things in doing what needs to be done.

- **Limit exposure** – If you must do something that really frightens you, do that action for 5 minutes and then turn away from it. You may even start by doing it for 60 seconds and then walking away. As you do this, add more time and sooner than later, you will no longer be afraid of it.

- **Ask for help** – Force yourself to ask for assistance. Know that asking for help does not make you weak. Those with anxiety typically despise asking for help it works wonders and you can gain a lot of insight.

- **Avoid distractions** – There are going to be times that you will just have to roll over distractions in order to not bump into procrastination. Turn off your phone, your computer, your T.V., etc, if need be. Get as much done as you can for as long as you can.

The goal of successfully beating procrastination as an anxiety sufferer is to take a leap of faith into the unknown. Is it scary? Hell yes, it is. But I promise, it's more worth it than standing around and watching your life pass right before your eyes.

Time-Management Skills to Avoid Procrastination

The 52/17 Technique

After many studies, it has actually been proven that many workers who are successfully productive work great for 52 minutes and then rest for 17 minutes in order to prepare for the next 52 minutes of uninterrupted activity. The simplicity of this rule makes it easy for anyone to incorporate it into their day to get the most out of it. This is best for jobs that require one to have intense mental focus and need to pay close attention to detail.

- Work 52 minutes with no interruptions or distractions with 100% motivated dedication to the task.

- Take a 17-minute break. Don't do anything that takes too much thought.

The Pomodoro Technique

This method totally eliminates the opportunity for disruptions by creating a work time of 25 minutes. This method allows those to avoid feeling overworked by taking breaks, which leads to more enhanced productivity.

- Pick a task that needs to be done right away.

- Dedicate 25 minutes of uninterrupted time on the tasks.

- If distractions or interruptions happen, jot them down and deal with them at a later time.

- When 25 minutes is up, take a 5-minute break.

- After every 4 working sessions of 25 minutes, take a longer break.

Manage Tasks on Paper

If you wish to get a lot done, prepare thoroughly. Write down every single step that will aid in getting the job done ahead of time. Make sure to break down the task into portions before starting. Writing out each part in detail allows your brain to prepare in advance, which will yield procrastination for standing in your way.

Prepare for Each Task

Now that you have listed each portion of a task, prepare for each portion in detail. When you start a task, make sure you have everything you need so that you will not have to get up and become distracted. Being prepared motivates you to get the task done much more efficiently.

Take Small Steps to Manage Tasks

Utilize the 80/20 rule which states that 20% of the task accounts for 80% of the value of that task. Once you take small steps to start a task, you will find that you will continue to take the actions to complete a task until accomplished.

"Slice" Tasks

You wouldn't go and try to eat an entire salami at once, right? Same goes with trimming down a job. The best way to complete bigger jobs is to slice them into pieces so that you can eat each piece at a time and savor it. With each slice, you can properly discipline yourself to get it done.

Start with a 5 Minute Task

You should treat a task like a block of Swiss cheese. Sounds absurd, but hear me out. Select a job that will take 5 minutes first and do not worry yourself about the job in its entirety. If you are writing a book, for example, break it up into small chunks that take a smaller amount of time to complete. Write one page. Research just one chapter and then write.

Perform the Tasks That Cause You Fear

Even though it is easier said than done, completing tasks that scare you first will give you the confidence to conquer the rest and is far more effective than saving them for last.

Do Unpleasant Tasks First

It's best to get the tasks you are not looking forward to out of the way first. This way, you have the rest of the day to look forward to instead of resenting the other terrible things you must get done later that day when you have less energy.

Quick Tips to Erase Procrastination Every Day

Habits are actions we all do each day without always consciously realizing it. Procrastination itself is a habit that is formed over time, for we are not born with it. In order to conquer procrastination, it is vital to form positive and productive habits that aid in helping you become the best person you can be and making the most of the 24 hours we all get each day.

Move it

One of the best and easiest habits we can incorporate into our everyday lives is to gather a change of scenery on a regular basis. Instead of collecting dust as we sit in front of our televisions, laptops, or phones, get up and stretch! Jog in place, perform pushups. Move till you can feel a shift in your frame of mind.

Set Reminders

Set up hourly and/or daily reminders that tell you when you should be working on something. This will combat wasted time in a jiffy! You can also set up reminders to include quotes that you find inspirational and motivating.

Grab a Motivation Buddy

There is something fantastic about having someone you know that helps you reach your goals, encourages you, and makes sure you are getting the things you need to accomplish. Having someone to keep you in line is a great motivator.

Accountability

Whether you want to make yourself accountable with the help of just yourself or with that of others, it is a great way to stay motivated. Social media has made it easy to put your goals out there for the public eye to see, to inspire others and for others to hold you accountable for achieving your goals.

Create Something Each Day

No matter what, make sure to attempt to create something daily. Write in a journal, draw or paint, make a video, learn a new skill. Anything that you enjoy that get creative juices flowing also fuels motivation, which fends off procrastination.

Wake Up Earlier

While many of us enjoy that extra hour of beauty rest, getting up just a bit earlier each morning not only gives you more time to get some more things done, but it also builds your overall confidence because of the simple fact you can get more things completed in a days' time. Also, the A.M. hours when you first wake up are the hours in which you are the most alert, which make for a great time to perform tasks that take a lot of focus.

Go To Bed Earlier

This habit goes hand-in-hand with getting up earlier. If you are getting up earlier, then you obviously will have to hit the hay a bit earlier as well. You need adequate sleep to keep up a sharp mind.

Clean As You Go

Procrastination seems to be a good excuse when it comes to cleaning our environments. Spend a few minutes each day cleaning, or clean as you go. This will keep piles and loads of things from becoming daunting.

Just Do It

We all make up excuses, but many of the things we have to do during the day boil down to just getting it done already. So be like Nike, and Just DO IT.

Avoid Emails

Especially at work, one of the worst habits is constantly checking email. Put out a task list and follow it first. Make a specific time to check email each day.

Eliminate Social Networks

Let's face it. Social media is quite a distraction. During the day, when you have things to get accomplished, turn them off and save checking them for afterward.

Time Yourself

Set up specific allotments of time to perform tasks. After each set amount of time, rest and then set a timer again and get back to the task. Try to do these things until you complete your task.

Track Yourself

One of the best ways to beat procrastination is to track yourself and see how much time you spend on certain things. There are a number of apps that you can utilize for this. (Discussed in the last chapter)

Create A Playlist

Beat procrastination with some tunes. Make a specific playlist full of music that helps you get motivated.

Realize "Perfect" Is Not real

Once you accept the fact that nothing in life is perfect, you can complete tasks with more confidence and at a much faster pace as well.

Be Mindful

Consciously knowing what you are doing at all time will help you to conquer procrastination and laziness. Don't get stuck in a rut of mindless activities. Be aware of your surroundings and the things you are doing as often as you can.

Set Daily Goals

Identify what you wish to get done at the start of each day. I recommend writing down at least three things. Break down tasks as you see fit. Work on them throughout the day until they are all completed.

Take Breaks

It's important not to be too hard on yourself, no matter how daunting that to-do list seems. We are all humans and if you negatively stew over uncompleted things, you will not get near as much as you can do. Breaks allow us time to re-coop and then get back to the nitty-gritty of a task.

Entertainment

Go to a museum. See a play. Watch a movie. While these things seem counterproductive to getting things done, in order to stay continuously motivated, it is important to refuel our creativeness.

Work Less

We procrastinate because of our plates are full. Learn to identify projects that need to be done first and complete those accordingly. If you feel overwhelmed, you will not work or function near as well.

Save Time for "Quiet Time"

In the modern society, we are always plugged into the world in some form or another. It can cause us stress without us even realizing it. Give yourself at the very least 15 minutes of time to refocus and give yourself a breather from the music, sounds, and talk of the world around you.

Don't Settle

You are not lazy. Laziness is not who you are and it never has to be a part of you. You can beat it if you really want to!

Erase Negativity with Mini Habits

Just after Christmas, a couple years ago, I was reflecting. I realized that I had tons of room to improve but always failed at keeping up with my New Year's resolutions. Instead, I decided that in 2017, I would explore other options.

On the 28th of December, I made the choice that I wanted to get back in shape. Previously, I hardly, if ever, exercised and had a consistent guilt about it. My goal was a 30-minute workout, realistic, right?

I found myself unmotivated, tired, and the guilt made me feel worthless. It wasn't until a few days later that I came across a small blog article about thinking the opposite of the ideas you are stuck on. The clear opposite of my 30-minute workout goal was chilling on the couch, stuffing my face with junk food, but my brain went to the idea of 'size.'

What if, instead of carrying that guilty feeling around all the time, I just performed one push-up? I know, right? How *absurd* of me to think that a single push-up would do anything to help me towards my goal.

What I found was a magical secret to unlocking my potential. When I found myself struggling with my bigger goals, I gave in and did a push-up. Since I was already down on the floor, I did a few more. Once I performed a few, my muscles felt warmed up and I decided to attempt a pull-up. As you can imagine, I did several more. And soon, I exercised for an entire 30 minutes!

What Are Mini Habits?

These habits are just like they sound. You choose a habit you want to change and you shrink them down to stupidly small tasks.

For instance, if you want to start writing at least 1,000 words per day:

- Write 50 words per day

- Read two pages of a book per day

Easy, right? I could accomplish this in 10 to 20 minutes or so. You will find that once you start meeting these daily requirements, you will far exceed them faster than you would imagine.

What is more essential than Your Habits?

You might be wondering how you can become more comfortable in your skin and be yourself in a cruel world with these so-called mini habits. Well, think about it. What is more important than the things you do each and every day? Nothing. Habits are responsible for 45% of how we behave, making up the foundation of *who we are* and how *happy* we are in life.

The main reason people fail to change anything in their life, even the aspects they *know* need to change is because they never instill new habits. Why? Simply because, in the past, they have tried to do way too much all at once. If establishing a new habit requires you to have more willpower than you can muster, you are bound to be unsuccessful. If a habit requires less willpower, you are much more likely to succeed!

Benefits of Mini Habits

There are many additional benefits that come with utilizing mini habits in your everyday life. Here are a few:

- Consistent success breeds more success
- No more guilt
- Stronger productivity

- Formation of more positively impactful habits
- Generation of motivation

Conclusion

I want to personally congratulate you for making it through the entirety of *Cognitive Behavioral Therapy Guide & Workbook Made Simple*.

With the conclusion of this book, I first want to give you a few personal homework assignments to really jumpstart your journey into a more positive, fulfilling life.

1. Go back and reread PART TWO. I know, I am asking a lot here! But to sincerely begin making core changes to your life, you first need to truthfully identify the issues you are currently living with.

   a. Open a Word document, jot on a piece of paper, whatever suits you. Answer these questions honestly:

      - What is something new you learned in Chapter 4: The Basics of Anxiety and Depression? Do you believe you exhibit these symptoms? If so, jot them down.

      - What are a few thoughts that naturally pop into your mind during the course of an average day in your life? These can be both negative and positively driven.

- What do you think causes you to automatically think these thoughts? How do you typically react towards them?

2. Now that you have written out a few likely very personal antidotes about your thoughts and actions, now take the time to reread PART THREE.

    a. Use a separate piece of paper or open a new Word document to jot down your answers:

    - What did you learn from each chapter? What new ideas set them apart from the advice you have been previously given or have read?

    - Write in detail the pessimistic thought that intrudes your life. When do they come about? Why do you think they do?

    - What are your core beliefs that you truly live by? How long have they been your beliefs? Are they *truly* yours?

- What are the ways of achieving positive mindfulness that you enjoyed and think you can actually implement in your life?

I want to pat you on the back for finishing this book and completing the above homework assignments! The fact that you are motivated to changing your life and mindset for the better says so much about your character! This will make a world of difference in the months to come as you fight against negativity and embrace positivity and change.

Even changing for the better is difficult to manage. That said, I remind you to be gentle with yourself as you venture into a more positive outlook and as you completely change your lease on life.

Now what? The next step is to take the abundance of knowledge you have acquired from reading this book and put it into practice in your everyday life. The best way to make any change, big or small, is to start making baby-like strides. This will help you to succeed faster as you eliminate darkness and embrace a much lighter mindset.

- Instead of becoming automatically overwhelmed when assigned big projects at work or home, look at them differently. Break them down into bite-sized chunks and complete each task, one at a time. You will fulfill that project with positivity still intact.

- Tough times in your relationship? Don't talk bad about your significant other, family member, or friend to others. This will just wreak more havoc. Instead, nip the issues you have with them in the bud. Talk to them personally and erase any bad feelings/actions. It will feel as if a boulder is lifted from you.

- Have you fallen into rough financial waters? What are the small steps you can take to get you back afloat?

As you have learned, cognitive behavioral therapy is made up of small but important pieces that help you to change your entire outlook of how you perceive life each day. When done correctly, you will notice that life ultimately gets better and is really is not how you have cracked it up to be.

A long conclusion, but I wanted to leave you with a few thoughts before you put this knowledge away and never use it! It is important to take care of yourself, both physically and mentally, for they both go hand-in-hand to determine the kind of life you lead.

I hope this book was not only informative but a good time to read, and that it was able to provide you with all of the tools you need to achieve your goals to live a happier, more fulfilled life!

Finally, if you found this book useful in any way, a review on Amazon is always appreciated!

Made in the USA
Middletown, DE
23 July 2019